World of Art

Anne Massey graduated in the History of Art and Design at the University of North... gained her doctorate there in 1984 w... Independent Group and post-war Brit... She has written extensively on the history of art and design, and her books include *The Independent Group: Modernism and Mass Culture in Britain, 1945–59* (1996); *Hollywood Beyond the Screen: Design and Material Culture* (2000); *Designing Liners: A History of Interior Design Afloat* (2006); *Chair* (2011); and *ICA 1946–68* (2014). Her co-edited books include *Interior Lives: Biography and the Interior* (2013) and *Pop Art and Design* (2017). She was the founding editor of the journal *Interiors: Design, Architecture, Culture* (2010–).

1 Victor Horta: top floor, Tassel house, Ixelles, Brussels, 1893. Horta's first design in an entirely new style. A glazed roof with slender iron supports provides brightly lit interiors. Instead of the usual Belgian corridors, Horta uses a central hall and staircase, heralding the modern movement's use of flowing spaces and 'plan of volumes'. Horta's whiplash line flies freely through the ironwork and over the walls, floor and ceiling.

World of Art

Interior Design Since 1900

Anne Massey

Fourth edition

First published in 1990 in the United Kingdom
by Thames & Hudson Ltd, 181A High Holborn,
London WC1V 7QX

www.thamesandhudson.com

First published in 1990 in the United States
of America by Thames & Hudson Inc.,
500 Fifth Avenue, New York, New York 10110

www.thamesandhudsonusa.com

This new edition 2020

Interior Design Since 1900 © 1990, 1996, 2008
and 2020 Thames & Hudson Ltd, London

Art direction and series design: Kummer & Herrman

British Library Cataloguing-in-Publication Data
A catalogue record for this book is available from
the British Library

Library of Congress Control Number 2019940739

ISBN 978-0-500-20460-3

Printed and bound in China through Asia Pacific
Offset Ltd

Contents

Preface

This new edition of *Interior Design Since 1900* provides an opportunity to reflect on the subject since the book's first appearance as *Interior Design of the 20th Century* in 1990. The original Foreword signalled the breadth of interior design as a subject, covering the areas of architecture, decoration, design and fine art within the context of social and economic history. This broad coverage remains at the heart of this updated account of recent interior design. The book's approach combines my knowledge of the history of architecture and design with my experience of practice working in my father's architectural firm and within the art and design school environment. As a practice, interior design covers so many areas of specialism from issues of sustainability and selecting the best services and materials through to understanding the subtleties of human belonging and emotion. It is this breadth that continues to make the subject so fascinating. Since the publication of the first edition, interior design has been the subject of increased academic attention, with the establishment of the academic journal *Interiors: Design, Architecture, Culture* and expanding interest in the popular media. This survey includes the work of professional architects, interior designers and interior decorators as well as the world of amateur design and decoration. The wealth of contemporary media coverage devoted to interior design makeovers, available styles and materials attest to the significance of our surroundings at home and in public spaces. The successful interior can provide comfort, promote psychological wellbeing, increase efficiency or promote a brand. Interiors also have the capacity to signal exclusion or jar the senses.

Style remains an important consideration in the study and understanding of interior design: for example, interior designers need to understand the historic traces they are working with during the repurposing of existing buildings or recreating interiors from the past, as exemplified by recent building in China and the Middle East. Amateur designers may need a knowledge of past styles to select the most appropriate look for their own projects. This volume begins its account of the narrative of style with the development of Victorian eclecticism, particularly as applied to the domestic interior as a refuge from the new and threatening world of modernity beyond the parlour and the front door. The fetishization of comfort in the home plus rules of etiquette and behaviour were key features of the Victorian domestic interior. But these structures of feeling were to be challenged by design reformers who collectively harked back to the medieval past as a way of improving interior design. A.W.N Pugin, followed by William Morris and the arts and crafts movement, endeavoured to educate popular taste through the written word and their own design practices.

This was a movement based in Great Britain and subsequently in North America, but this Western dominance was challenged with the opening up of trade with Japan in the later nineteenth century. The trans-cultural exchange between East and West led to the creation of the aesthetic-movement style that glorified the sparse and elegant style of Japan. In turn this led to the global phenomenon of art nouveau, which flourished throughout Europe, including Scandinavia and Russia, as well as the United States. The organic, whiplash curve and innovative use of metal, glass and wood symbolized the start of a new century.

Modern methods of printing and production from the beginning of the twentieth century onwards meant that interior design styles could circulate globally and be quickly adopted around the world. This is particularly true of the most prevalent style to affect interior design since 1900, that of modernism. The leading architects of the modern movement ensured that their message of form follows function and minimalism in everyday living reached a wide audience through manifestos, illustrated magazines and avant-garde practice. Modern architects including Le Corbusier, Ludwig Mies van der Rohe and Walter Gropius were self-appointed pioneers of a new style for the design of every aspect of life. The driving force behind this spare, geometric style was to promote cleanliness and hygiene rather than comfort. Decoration was anathema to the modern movement and their designs for public and private interiors alike. This could be regarded as excessively controlling, as the clients and end-users of modern buildings were left with little scope to personalize their surroundings. As authors such as Penny Sparke (*The Modern Interior*, 2008) and Hilde Heynen and G. Baydar (*Negotiating Domesticity: Spatial Productions of Gender in Modern Architecture*, 2005) have argued, this dominance over the domestic on behalf of modern architects was not without its problems. It could be argued that this drive for rationalism in the design of interiors was anti-*gemütlich* and had an anti-feminine dimension to it.

In direct contrast to modernism, the art deco style of the 1920s and 1930s celebrated femininity, glamour and surface decoration. This was a popular, commercial style and was used for homes, cinemas and offices throughout the world. From Miami Beach to Napier in New Zealand, and from Mumbai to Asmara in Africa, this style signified pleasure and frivolity. It was associated with Hollywood cinema and jazz music, ancient Egypt and modern materials. Art deco has been constantly revived ever since as the signifier of luxury and hedonism, whether on cruise ships or in bars and restaurants around the world. Many of the original art deco sites have been awarded UNESCO's World Heritage status to preserve them and protect them from redevelopment.

The first four chapters of this edition establish the vocabulary of style as an important theme, from Victorian eclecticism, the arts and crafts movement, art nouveau, the modern movement and art deco. With this story of interior design styles mapped out, attention is then turned to the creative professionals involved in interior design – the interior decorator and designer. The fifth chapter charts the development of interior decoration as a profession in the United States and beyond. While the history of modern architecture is dominated by the hero, usually male, architect, the history of interior decoration is the domain of the female and queer practitioner. Recent work by John Potvin has tracked the queer design history of interior decoration which has been overlooked for too long. In his *Bachelors of a Different Sort: Queer Aesthetics, Material Culture and the Modern Interior in Britain* (2014) he argued for the importance of a consideration of sexuality and identity in accounting for the history of interior decoration and the interior decorator.

The perennial history of modernism is then revisited in Chapter Six, with an examination of its increased dominance in the post-war world as the symbol of both democracy and socialism. The profession of interior design grew out of interior decoration and modern architecture in the 1950s and 1960s with new courses and professional organizations. The triangle of interior decoration, interior design and architecture presents a complex and fraught set of relationships that remain largely unresolved.

Another important aspect of interior design in addition to style and the designer is the end user or consumer. Chapter Seven examines the role of the inhabitant in the interior. It looks at the development of do-it-yourself and consumer culture in shaping the lived-in environment. Shopping habits began to change with the growth of a new building type, the supermarket and car ownership boomed. Colour and pattern marked the era of consumer culture in the 1950s and 1960s.

Conversely, the growth of consumer culture in the post-war economic boom inspired architects and designers in the creation of a pop sensibility in the shape of pop art and design. This was a youthful and colourful style that epitomized the swinging sixties and acted as a style and approach for teenage identity. A throwaway aesthetic, it epitomized an era when the ephemeral was valued in opposition to the permanence of modernist ethics. This challenge to modernism was furthered in the era of post-modernism, as Chapter Seven demonstrates. A mixture of past styles was ironically combined by groups such as the Italian outfit Memphis to present a more theoretically driven yet playful approach to interior design.

Post-modernism emerged at a time of economic prosperity in the West, and expressed an attitude of playfulness and wit. However, a dawning crisis in terms of global, environmental issues ushered in an era of concern for the sustainability of the design of the interior, and this is covered in Chapter Eight. New regulations in terms of materials, insulation and the recyclability of the stuff of interior design are now a feature of a new world of sustainability, if not basic survival. As the architect Jeremy Till has archly commented, architecture is but waste in transit (*Architecture Depends*, 2013). And the forms of modernism evolved into the aesthetic of minimalism in the interior, stripping out and paring back the perceived mess of human habitation. Interior design of the twenty-first century also has an ever-changing and complex relationship with technology, with digitally projected decoration and intelligent systems controlling services at our command from a smartphone or voice-activated controls. The digital presence is all but invisible, but style remains significant for interior design: even if there are no completely new styles to play with, what is left is unique combinations from the existing palette of possibilities.

Visual styles continue to represent different aspects of power, prestige and identity. And interior design can also be used to disrupt the status quo and insert new understandings of politics and society. The new additional chapter at the end of this edition takes the theme of 'Transnational Interiors'. It takes a post-colonial view of global interior design and looks beyond the usual Western range of examples to interior design in Africa and Asia. The modernist work of Le Corbusier is considered within an Indian context, with a consideration of the new capital city of Chandigarh in Punjab. The Sri Lankan designers Minnette de Silva and Geoffrey Bawa are then considered as figures critical of modernist tropical modernism. More recent buildings are then covered, including high-rise luxury flats and hotels in India and Dubai as examples of transnational interior design. The chapter also considers contemporary design in Africa as an important vehicle for establishing new national identities. The chapter also includes a consideration of the changing relationship between nature and the interior.

In modernist interiors the picture window indicated a controlling and superior view of the natural world, visible but separate. Recent developments in interior design display a more biophilic attitude. With the fashion for folding glazed doors in place of the picture window, the outside space of the private, usually rear, garden connects seamlessly with the interior. So popular is the theme of bringing the exterior into the interior that a British television series, *Inside Out Homes*, is devoted to blending the two. The contemporary interior can now mimic natural light at all times of the day with LED lights, whilst office atria are frequently decorated with a living wall of green vegetation.

This book charts the course of the new discipline of interior design through the twentieth century, into the twenty-first and right up until the present day. The themes of style, authorship, consumption and post-colonialism are all covered to tell this fascinating story of the designed, interior space.

Chapter 1
Reforming Victorian Taste

The most important design reform movement to affect the interior in the nineteenth century was that of the arts and crafts. Starting in Britain, the movement had a far-reaching influence on twentieth-century design.

The Industrial Revolution of the second half of the eighteenth century in Britain generated a totally new economic and social structure. The twin forces of industrialization and urbanization dictated a new way of life for the population as a whole. By the mid-nineteenth century, Britain led the world in terms of trade and enjoyed great prosperity. The foundation of a capitalist economy spawned a thriving middle class. Whereas previously decisions about the style of interiors had concerned chiefly the upper classes, who were advised by the architect, plasterer or upholsterer, this changed with the Industrial Revolution and the rise of a new bourgeoisie, anxious to communicate its newfound prosperity in terms of visual culture but insecure in its own taste.

The Victorian middle class generally settled on the edge of the city in new suburban estates. The appearance of the interiors of these modest three-storey homes and the way in which the inhabitants conducted themselves within were dictated by elaborate codes of behaviour. The numerous advice manuals dealing with social intercourse and interior decoration, starting with Mrs Beeton's *Book of Household Management,* first published in England in 1861, and Mrs E.B. Duffey's *What Women Should Know,* published in America in 1871, reveal how rigid and how crucial were the codes that governed the home. The precise etiquette for receiving guests, organizing dinner parties and managing the servants was all set down.

2 Working-class interior, c. 1900. Even in the least luxurious interior, decoration was important; witness the draped mantelshelf.

Items of household decoration such as wallpaper, textiles and carpets were now being mass produced and purchased for the first time by a bourgeoisie who emulated their social superiors with the furnishing of the formal drawing room. This was the room used to receive visitors, and usually had heavy curtains and thick lace at the windows, a patterned carpet, generously upholstered seating, ornate furniture and a huge range of ornaments, pictures and surface decoration. The overall impression needed to be one of comfort, richness and formality. Furniture could be bought from the new department stores, or in America by mail order. The seven-piece suite, manufactured and marketed in America during the 1870s by firms such as McDonough, Price and Co., used rich fabrics with added details like buttoning, tufting, pleating and fringing to create a sumptuous effect. The chairs used internal springing, popularized in France in the 1840s and common to most drawing-room seating by the 1850s, to provide a visual rather than merely physical effect of comfort. The springs had the advantage of returning the seat to the desired smooth shape after use. The ordering of the Victorian drawing room was governed by the need to impress, a need felt by even the working-class homemaker.

2

Reforming Victorian Taste

3 New York drawing room, photographed in 1894. The dominance of surface decoration, ostentatious upholstery and mixture of period styles are typical of the late nineteenth-century interior, here with French influence.

3   However all-pervasive the Victorian middle-class desire to express comfort and wealth, the aesthetic standard of the interior disturbed contemporary critics, and a large body of writing appeared during the nineteenth century to give advice on taste and interior design. Writers from A.W.N. Pugin (1812–1852) onwards equated what they regarded as 'good' design with high moral standards. Pugin led a campaign for the gothic style. His two books on the subject, *Contrasts* (1836) and the more detailed *The True Principles of Pointed or Christian Architecture* (1841), make a connection between his own Catholicism and the architecture of the late thirteenth to fifteenth centuries. For Pugin, gothic was an expression of a just and Christian society in contrast to nineteenth-century industrial society with its social ills. The Victorian gothic revival was mainly inspired by Pugin and his interiors for the new Houses of Parliament building designed by Sir Charles Barry (1795–1860). The style continued in use into the twentieth century, feeding into the arts and crafts movement.

The gothic style was revived to create a brilliant effect in the work of William Burges (1827–1881) for his wealthy and eccentric client, the Marquis of Bute. Burges created two gothic fantasies, Cardiff Castle (1868–81) and Castell Coch (1875–81), near Cardiff.

The lavish, boldly coloured decorations exemplify the Victorian tendency to romanticize the Middle Ages. The walls and ceilings were brightly painted, carved and gilded, and the rooms were embellished with carved and painted figures taken from ecclesiastical sources. The furniture designed by Burges is heavy, decorated with turrets and similar carving inspired by gothic architecture as well as furniture.

Pugin's work was an inspiration to the leading writer on art and design in nineteenth-century Britain, John Ruskin (1819–1900), who influenced taste in interior design through his writings on art in *The Times* newspaper and his books, such as *The Seven Lamps of Architecture* (1849) and *The Stones of Venice* (1851–3). He warned against the common practice of making one material look like another, and the effort to create a new style when gothic could not be surpassed. Like Pugin, he saw the ugliness that surrounded him as the unavoidable result of the miserable conditions for the majority brought by the Industrial Revolution. He took issue with the Victorian fashion for cramming as much as possible into a room to symbolize the owners' wealth and status, writing in *The Seven Lamps of Architecture:* '... but I would not have that useless expense on unnoticed fineries or formalities; cornicing of ceilings and graining of doors, and fringing of curtains, and thousands such; things which have become falsely and pathetically habitual – things on whose common appliance hang whole trades, to which there never yet belonged the blessing of giving one ray of real pleasure, or becoming of the remotest or most contemptible use – things which cause half the expense of life, and destroy more than half its comfort, manliness, respectability, freshness, and facility.'

'I know what it is', he continued, 'to live in a cottage with a deal floor and roof, and a hearth of mica slate; and I know it to be in many respects healthier and happier than living between a Turkey carpet and gilded ceiling, beside a steel grate and polished fender.'

Ruskin's critique of new, mass-produced furniture and furnishings was expressed again in a letter he wrote to *The Times* of 25 May 1854, in which he discusses William Holman Hunt's painting on the theme of adultery, *The Awakening Conscience* (1853), with reference to the 'fatal newness' of the interior. For Ruskin, moral virtue and such new furniture were incompatible.

Ruskin's rejection of mass-produced furniture and his advocacy of design from the past influenced a whole generation of writers and designers, most notably the socialist, designer and founder of the arts and crafts movement, William Morris

4 William Holman Hunt: *The Awakening Conscience*, 1853. For Ruskin, the painting's theme of the 'love nest' was expressed largely in terms of the garish and shiny furnishings, for instance the ill-matched 'painted' veneer on the piano-end.

(1834–1896). Morris established interior design and the production of furniture and furnishings as a valid enterprise for the architect and fine artist, firing the arts and crafts movement of the 1880s to 'Turn our artists into craftsmen and our craftsmen into artists!' After studying theology

5 Hallway of the Red House, Bexleyheath, built by Philip Webb for William Morris and his bride in 1859–60. Webb's simple staircase and hall cupboard are gothic in inspiration. The cupboard doors are painted with scenes of Arthurian romance by the artist Burne-Jones.

at Exeter College, Oxford, Morris decided against a life as a clergyman, became interested in architecture, and worked in the offices of the gothic revival architect G.E. Street (1824–1881) before abandoning the profession to become an artist. This career too proved abortive, and after his marriage to Jane Burden in 1859 he concentrated on design.

Morris commissioned his new home, the Red House at Bexleyheath, Kent (1859–60), from a former colleague in Street's practice, Philip Webb (1831–1915). When the house was complete, Morris and his circle of friends, which included Webb, Dante Gabriel Rossetti (1828–1882) of the Pre-Raphaelite Brotherhood and the young artist Edward Burne-Jones (1833–1898), decorated the interior in a style that harmonized with Webb's vernacular building, a modest English country house of red brick which incorporated medieval and seventeenth-century features at a time when late Georgian and Italianate forms were the norm. Morris was unique in consciously matching interior to exterior so completely in an unpretentious house. The architectural fitments were sturdy and simple compared with mainstream Victorian design. Oak rather than rich mahogany was used throughout the house, for the staircase, beams and furniture. The red-tiled hall reflected the red-brick exterior and brick chimneypieces. All the textiles were designed and hand-crafted by Morris and his circle, and the furniture such as the chest in the entrance hall was hand-painted by Burne-Jones.

6

Like Ruskin, Morris detested the mass-produced household goods of the age and equated them with the atrocious living and factory conditions endured by the working classes. He believed strongly that good design could only be produced by men and women working creatively with their hands.

Although a convinced Marxist, Morris was also a successful entrepreneur. He founded the firm Morris, Marshall, Faulkner & Co. in 1861 to design and produce well-made textiles, furniture and carpets, building on the success of the Red House interior. In 1875 the firm became Morris & Co. with Morris as sole proprietor, and went on to produce the hand block-printed wallpapers and textiles whose designs are still popular today. One of Morris & Co.'s most important design commissions was for the Green Dining Room (1865–7) at the South Kensington Museum, London (now the Victoria and Albert Museum). The overall scheme for the refreshment room was by Webb, who was responsible for the Japanese-inspired embossed plaster sections on the upper part of the walls. Renaissance-inspired stained glass and dado panels were by Burne-Jones. Later domestic interior design commissions include 'Clouds' at East Knoyle in Wiltshire (1879–91) for the Hon. Percy Wyndham and Wightwick Manor in Staffordshire, one of the finest of the surviving interiors. But what was Morris's influence on subsequent interior design?

The ethical approach of Morris and his circle inspired a network of craft guilds, small groups of artist-designers such as that of C.R. Ashbee (1863–1942), whose Guild of Handicraft was founded in the East End of London in 1888 and moved to Chipping Campden, Gloucestershire, in 1902 in a utopian attempt to live out the Morris ideal of crafts production in a rural community. The Art-Workers' Guild was another such group, founded in 1884 as an alternative to the architecturally based Royal Institute of British Architects and the fine art Royal Academy. Its architects and craftspeople, who admired Ruskin and Morris, included the designers Walter Crane (1845–1915) and Lewis F. Day (1845–1910) and the architect W.R. Lethaby (1857–1931). The Guild provided an important platform for the public discussion of craft techniques and style but was not concerned with actual production. Some of the members of the Guild went on to found the Arts and Crafts Exhibition Society, which organized shows of arts and crafts work from 1888 onwards.

Morris inspired not only design reform but also new methods of training designers by hand-making objects, where previously design and manufacture had been two separate processes. The greatest achievement of W.R. Lethaby was the founding of the London Central School of Arts and Crafts in 1894, the first art school to have teaching workshops for crafts.

It was through the influence of Ruskin and Morris that furnishing an interior with newly acquired antiques became fashionable for the first time. The Sussex Chair attributed to Rossetti and produced by Morris & Co. was a recreation of an earlier vernacular model. When Rossetti moved to a new house in Chelsea, London, in 1862, however, he chose to furnish it largely with old furniture of different periods and in different styles. The key point for the arts and crafts movement of the 1880s was that a chair, whether from the seventeenth or nineteenth century, should be manifestly handmade, with the joints visible. The more clearly expressed the construction the more honest the piece, and the greater the contrast with the machine-carved, highly polished veneers of mainstream taste. This led to an 'antiques movement' that gained momentum in the late nineteenth century and was supported by specialist dealers and published furniture histories.

6 Morris advocated the use of wall-hangings and of simple furniture based on country models. The walls of his own drawing room at Kelmscott House, Hammersmith, c. 1880, were hung with his 'Bird' tapestry; the adjustable Morris & Co. chair on the left was developed c. 1866 from a Sussex type, while the settle from the Red House by Philip Webb is both rural and medieval in style.

However, Morris's and the arts and crafts' main influence on subsequent interior design was largely formal, as opposed to ethical. The 'honest' furniture of Morris & Co. was expensive and had a limited circulation. Morris was a highly talented designer of flat patterns, and the interweaving lines and forms drawn from nature of the *Tulip* chintz of 1875 and the *Cray* chintz of 1884, for example, would inspire designers in Britain and America and on the Continent.

C.F.A. Voysey (1857–1941) was an architect of the next generation who designed houses and their interiors with the arts and crafts regard for the vernacular and honest workmanship, and extended his interest to designing wallpapers, textiles, carpets and furniture for his schemes. His own house, The Orchard, Chorleywood, Hertfordshire (1899), has plain interiors with inglenooks (large fireplace recesses) and unpretentious furniture based on English vernacular models. His daring use of scale, however, influenced the architect-designer Charles Rennie Mackintosh (Chapter 2). Voysey's door in the hall of The Orchard reaches above the low picture rail, and the effect of breadth is exaggerated by heart-tipped metal hinges that almost span the door. A second feature is that the woodwork and ceiling of The Orchard were painted white, and this, combined with the expanses of window glass, particularly

7 C.F.A. Voysey: entrance hall of The Orchard, Chorleywood, 1899. Voysey's self-consciously simple, sparse interiors reflected arts and crafts ideals, and were widely influential on the Continent.

8 M.H. Baillie Scott's colourful design for a Music Room, part of the winning competition entry for 'The House of an Art Lover', 1901.

in the dining room, made the interiors appear bright and even glaring by the standards of earlier Victorian taste. Voysey's evident belief in the benefits of stark, honest interiors and furniture is overriding. Voysey's contemporary, the architect Mackay Hugh Baillie Scott (1865–1945), employs more colour and decorative detail in his domestic interiors, for example stained glass in the windows and stencilling on the walls.

Baillie Scott's influential article for *The Studio* of January 1895 entitled 'An Ideal Suburban House' included plans for an adventurous layout. A large, high, medieval-style hall has a music gallery on the first floor and an inglenook on the wall opposite, formed by an overhanging passage. Unusually, folding screens divide the rooms. Baillie Scott realized much of the plan in 'An Ideal Suburban House' at the White House, Helensburgh (1899–1900), and went on to further commissions in Europe and America after publication of his work in *The Studio.* In 1901 he won a competition organized by Alexander Koch, the German publisher of *Innen Dekoration* magazine, to design 'The House of an Art Lover'. The painted woodwork and emphasis on the vertical, particularly in the Music Room, link the design with art nouveau.

Baillie Scott was also successful in the less prestigious Letchworth Cheap Cottages competition in 1905. Letchworth Garden City in Hertfordshire was one of several housing developments built to provide functional and healthy homes for the working classes in economical arts and crafts style. Other Garden City schemes include Hampstead Garden Suburb, begun in 1907 to the north of London and overseen by architect Sir Edwin Lutyens (1869–1944). Lutyens established his career at the turn of the century as a designer of medium-sized country houses in the arts and crafts style. Deanery Gardens, Sonning, Berkshire (1899–1901), is half-timbered outside, while inside there are exposed beams, white plaster walls and bare floorboards. At this date such a design could no longer be considered revolutionary. The radical overtones of vernacular architecture and simple hand-crafted furniture were slowly yielding to the complex and enduring ideology of Britain as a nation with a remote and romanticized rural past.

9

9 Edwin Lutyens: sitting room, Deanery Gardens, Sonning, 1901. Jacobean-style furniture, bare oak floorboards, oak panelling and exposed beams evoke an 'Old English' rural atmosphere, redolent of solidity and craftsmanship.

10 Plain oak furniture made by Gordon Russell at Broadway, Worcestershire, 1925. Simple country styles remained current throughout most of the twentieth century.

The arts and crafts movement had little effect on design on the Continent until the 1890s, when it contributed to the creation of art nouveau and the beginnings of the modern movement. American interior design, however, was profoundly influenced by the reforming ethics and naturalistic style of Morris and his followers, which chimed with the frontier spirit and sense of individualism that were growing stronger as America began to establish a national identity in design. Organizations were founded on English models, including the American Art Workers' Guild in 1885, the Chicago Arts and Crafts Society in 1897 and the Minneapolis Arts and Crafts Society in 1899. Americans learned of British trends through lecture tours by leading theorists, particularly the designer Christopher Dresser (1834–1904) in 1876 and C.R. Ashbee in 1896 and 1900. The magazine *The Studio* was published in America as the *International Studio,* and news of British design dominated American periodicals such as *House Beautiful,* started in 1896, and *The Craftsman,* which had been founded by the American arts and crafts designer Gustav Stickley (1858–1942) in 1901 following an extensive visit to Europe. Morris & Co. goods were exported to America and stocked by the Marshall Field Wholesale Store in Chicago.

Charles Sumner Greene (1868–1957), of the American architectural partnership Greene and Greene, had travelled

11–12

11–12 Gustav Stickley: reclining chair of c. 1902 and settee of 1905–7. Stickley's furniture in the so-called 'Craftsman style' enthusiastically followed the teaching of Morris and other English arts and crafts designers, in that the wood is left plain and the joints are visible. At the same time, Stickley believed his designs were particularly suited to what he described as 'the fundamental sturdiness and directness of the American point of view'.

13 Léon Jallot: dining room, Brittany, 1926. Arts and crafts influence awakened designers to the value of the rural heritage.

14 Living room, David B. Gamble House, Pasadena, 1908, by Greene and Greene. Beautifully finished woodwork and stained glass represent the Californian version of arts and crafts. Japanese influence appears in the chair-backs and jointed timbers of the inglenook.

to Britain to learn more of the arts and crafts movement at first hand, as well as gleaning information from *International Studio*. With his brother Henry Mather Greene (1870–1954) he designed four important arts and crafts houses in California for the Blackers, Gambles, Pratts and Maybecks between 1907 and 1909. The inner wooden frame of David B. Gamble House, Pasadena (1908), is clearly articulated, with beautifully finished pegged joints providing a visual feature and evidence of the work of a team of highly skilled craftsmen supervised on site by the architects. Extensive use was made of leaded coloured glass for windows, doors and light fittings, all of which were designed by the architects, as was the hand-crafted furniture. Greene and Greene made an important departure from British arts and crafts house-plans by including terraces, verandahs and courtyards that integrated the interior and garden. However, the debt to William Morris and the British domestic revival, which began with Webb's Red House and continued in the work of Voysey and Baillie Scott, remains predominant.

14

15 Omega Workshops: decoration of Charleston Farmhouse, Sussex, 1920s. Walls, screens, cupboards and even the log-box were painted by the artists.

William Morris's ideal that there should be an obvious artistic presence in the interior continued to influence interior decorators throughout the twentieth century. In Britain, the Omega Workshops founded by the art critic Roger Fry in 1913 set out to bring the talents of the painter to the domestic interior. Artists Duncan Grant and Vanessa Bell joined Fry in painting decorations onto mundane and often badly made pieces of furniture, and printing fabrics with bold designs based on the work of Henri Matisse. Charleston Farmhouse in Sussex, which the Bloomsbury Group bohemians used as a country retreat, had every flat surface painted by one of the group with strong colour combinations and bold post-impressionist forms. During the 1980s the fashion and furnishing-fabric retailer Laura Ashley launched a range of wallpapers and fabrics based on Bell's and Grant's designs.

Middle European arts and crafts movements gathered momentum during the 1890s, and were still in evidence at the 1925 Paris Exposition des Arts Décoratifs. The Polish Pavilion

15

by Joseph Czajkowski was decorated with brightly coloured paintings inspired by folk art, and the Greeks displayed a 'Greek Peasant Dwelling'.

William Morris's designs also inspired the aesthetic movement of the late 1860s and 1870s, an alternative style of reformist design in Britain that was to have a great influence in America. The other principal inspiration for the aesthetic movement was Japanese design. This had first been seen by the British public at the 1862 International Exhibition in London when the British Consul in Tokyo, Rutherford Alcock, exhibited a collection of Japanese artefacts. The simplicity and exoticism of blue and white porcelain, silks and lacquerwork appealed to British designers craving an alternative to mass-produced revivalism and opulence. Much of the Japanese display was bought by the firm of Farmer and Rogers, who used it to stock their 'Oriental Warehouse' selling Japanese silks, prints and lacquer. Arthur Lasenby Liberty (1843–1917) was employed by the firm in 1862, and in 1875 he bought its entire Japanese stock of goods and opened his own 'Oriental Bazaar' to sell the popular *japonisme*. Soon afterwards he opened Liberty, the shop that went on to

16 Fashionable bedroom by Liberty, 1897. Light, elegantly patterned fabrics and wallpapers, a delicate Queen Anne Revival table, a metal (rather than a wooden) bedstead for health and ease of cleaning, all express the reforming aims of the arts and crafts and aesthetic movements.

establish the exclusive 'Liberty & Co.' look, supplying oriental ceramics and textiles with British-designed metalwork and furniture for the creation of fashionable interiors.

The aesthetic movement lacked the moral concerns of the arts and crafts movement. Its object was to create less ponderous and healthier 'artistic' interiors for the Victorian middle classes, whose tastes had now matured. One of the architect-designers of the movement, R.W. Edis (1839–1927), advised in his book *Healthy Furniture and Decoration* (1884) against the use of 'jarring colours and patterns' in the bedroom, as these would tend to cause 'nervous irritability'. Despite the concern for health, the slogan 'Art for Art's sake' sums up the movement's preoccupations, in contrast with the political aspirations of William Morris. The short-lived Century

17 'Art Furniture' in its setting. R.W. Edis's illustration of his own drawing room with painted frieze, Morris & Co. wallpaper, chair (on the left) designed by William Godwin, and cupboard for china, painted with four heads representing the Seasons.

18 Century Guild stand at the Liverpool International Exhibition in 1886, with furniture by Mackmurdo of slender forms and Japanese inspiration.

18

Guild, founded by A.H. Mackmurdo (1851–1942) in 1882, shared Morris's convictions in attempting to bring fine art into the sphere of everyday life. The Guild designed and exhibited furniture, textiles and wallpapers that mingled naturalistic ornament such as Morris had used with the slender forms and bold colours of Japan.

19

The early houses of architect Richard Norman Shaw (1831–1912) had much in common with the arts and crafts movement, often providing warm panelled interiors with inglenooks and heavy oak furniture, for example at Cragside, Northumberland (1870–85), the first house, incidentally, to be lit by hydro-electricity. At the same time Shaw was pioneering a very different style of architecture, known as Queen Anne, to provide a light, comfortable and elegant type of home. Old Swan House, Chelsea, London (1875–77), was furnished with reproduction Queen Anne tables, chairs and cupboards and Japanese blue-and-white ware. The key room was the living room on the first floor that ran the width of the street facade, thus incorporating three Queen Anne-style windows in one room.

Reforming Victorian Taste

19 Dining room inglenook in Richard Norman Shaw's Cragside, Northumberland, 1870–85. The carved inscription reads: 'East or West, Hame's Best', emphasizing a preoccupation with the domestic interior that would continue into the twentieth century. Art enters the home with Morris & Co. stained-glass windows by Burne-Jones. The gothic revival arch shelters a powerful industrialist, Sir William Armstrong, depicted at his ease in the guise of an enlightened country gentleman.

20   The epitome of aesthetic movement taste is the Peacock Room, created for the Liverpool shipping magnate and collector of Japanese ceramics Frederick Leyland. The artist James McNeill Whistler (1834–1903) painted the leather walls a startling turquoise with gold peacocks, the quintessential symbol of the movement. The large and exotic house in Kensington, London, designed for the fashionable artist Lord Leighton by George Aitchison (1825–1910), was unusual in having an Arab Court complete with fountain, lattice-work and Islamic tiles. The more modest town-house of graphic artist Linley Sambourne in Stafford Terrace, Kensington, London, was furnished by the

20 The epitome of aesthetic movement taste: the Peacock Room, a dining room with built-in shelving for the display of oriental porcelain, and panels in oriental style, painted a vivid blue by the artist James McNeill Whistler and decorated with golden peacocks and chrysanthemums.

occupant in the aesthetic style from 1874 onwards, and is now preserved by the Victorian Society. For the middle classes, the London suburb of Bedford Park was designed in 1870 by Norman Shaw and others as an estate for like-minded aesthetes.

A lecture tour by Oscar Wilde in 1882–3 acquainted the American public with fashionable English taste. Wilde's house in Tite Street, Chelsea, had recently been refurbished by the aesthetic movement architect E.W. Godwin (1833–1886), and he had learned of aesthetic movement principles from this source. Books also played a role in bringing British design to America. Charles Locke Eastlake's *Hints on Household Taste in Furniture, Upholstery and Other Details,* published in London in 1868, ran to seven editions in America from 1872 to 1890. Eastlake criticized the work of professional decorating firms, and castigated their encouragement of ephemeral trends: 'In the eyes of Materfamilias there was no upholstery which could possibly surpass that which the most fashionable upholsterer supplied... When did people first adopt the monstrous notion that the "Last pattern out" must be the best? Is good taste so rapidly progressive that every mug which leaves the potter's hands surpasses in shape the last which is moulded?'

Influenced by William Morris, Eastlake recommended antique furniture combined with his own gothic revival designs. These included sturdy chests, benches and bookcases decorated with pointed arches and carved gothic ornament. However, it was more the reforming spirit of his writing than the gothic style that caught the American imagination. His book made such an impact that 'Eastlake Furniture' or 'Art Furniture', based on his tenets of simple, good construction, was manufactured in America. Charles Tisch and the Herter Brothers produced such furniture in New York during the 1870s and 1880s.

21 Charles L. Eastlake's sideboard, unvarnished and functional, 'at first glance, proclaiming its real purpose', as illustrated in his best-selling *Hints on Household Taste* (1878 edn).

22 Louis Comfort Tiffany: library of the designer's own apartment, East 26th Street, New York, as illustrated in *Artistic Houses*, 1883.

The 'Artistic' interior became a mark of wealth, status and good taste in the 1880s. *Artistic Houses: Being a Series of Interior Views of a Number of the Most Beautiful and Celebrated Homes in the United States with a Description of the Art Treasures Contained Therein*, published in New York in 1883, featured key New York interiors in the aesthetic style. The designer Louis Comfort

22 Tiffany's flat on East 26th Street, New York, combined all the hallmarks of the aesthetic interior: Moorish motifs over the doors; Japanese wallpaper; Eastlake-inspired furniture; peacock feathers; and walls divided into four horizontal bands – the skirting board, dado, papered infill and frieze. Short-lived as the aesthetic movement was (and by the turn of the century it had died out both in the United States and Britain), the attitudes it inherited from William Morris – that art should play a role in the interior and that machine-production was undesirable – had an enduring effect on twentieth-century interior design and architecture. The naturalistic forms of Morris's surface patterns and *japonisme* were among the inspirations of the first great design style of the twentieth century, art nouveau.

Chapter 2
The Search for a New Style

The arts and crafts movement had widened the debate about what constituted good design, but had little effect on conventional interior design at the turn of the century, either in America or Europe. For the grander type of interior the prevalent style was the Beaux-Arts, so called because its source was in the teaching of the École des Beaux-Arts in Paris. This was a conservative style, inspired by French classical architecture of the seventeenth and eighteenth centuries, and in interior decoration was marked by lavish use of carving, gilding, rich marble and extravagant lighting, well suited to provide an atmosphere of grandeur for large hotels, department stores, opera houses and the ostentatious houses of the wealthy. A graduate of the École, Jean Louis Charles Garnier (1825–1898), created the best-known example of the style with the foyer of the Paris Opéra (1861–74). The wide, sweeping staircase, caryatids, polychrome marble, richly carved ornament in an exaggerated baroque style and sheer quantity of candelabra all contributed to a glittering effect.

23

The Paris Opéra and the Beaux-Arts style in general influenced interiors of opera houses, department stores, hotels, municipal buildings and private houses all over the world. This influence was most pronounced in America, where even after the First World War an average of fifteen American candidates each year sat the entrance examination for the École. The American Richard Morris Hunt (1827–1895) joined the École in 1846 (the first American to do so) and the academic training bore fruit when he returned to America in 1855 to design French Renaissance Revival mansions for millionaires such as W.K. Vanderbilt and J.J. Astor in New York and Long Island. The leading American architectural practice of McKim, Mead & White (1879–1915) owed a similar debt to the Beaux-Arts

23 Charles Garnier's staircase, Paris Opéra, 1861–74: a baroque version of the Beaux-Arts style. The international influence of the École continued right up to the Second World War, and interest in the French classical tradition was renewed in the 1970s with the advent of post-modernism.

tradition. One of the partners, Charles Follen McKim, trained at the École from 1867 to 1870, and the interiors of large public buildings such as the Boston Public Library (1887) and the Pierpont Morgan Library, New York (1903–6), as well as smaller domestic residences such as that of John Innes Kane, New York City, reveal an adherence to the academic principles taught at the École.

Splendid interiors by McKim, Mead & White are preserved at the Villard houses, Madison Avenue, New York (1883–5), designed as a group of residences for the railway magnate Henry Villard and his friends (now the public rooms of the Lotte New York Palace Hotel). The Gold Room is the most lavish. Originally intended as a music room, it is two storeys high with a balcony at the north end to accommodate the musicians. The decoration of the room was finished in 1886 when Whitelaw Reid bought the house and commissioned Stanford White (1853–1906) of McKim, Mead and White to oversee its completion. The coffered ceiling is ornately carved and gilded in the Renaissance manner. The American artist

The Search for a New Style

and designer John La Farge (1835–1910) filled the two large arches at the top of the north and south walls with paintings in an academic style, representing music and drama. Beneath are carved panels that reproduce those by Luca della Robbia in the Sacristy of Florence Cathedral. The rest of the wall-panelling is richly carved with musical instruments and garlands in low relief. Such heavy reliance on classical models and grand, expensive decoration is typical of the Beaux-Arts.

In Britain the firm of Mewès and Davis (1900–14) were the leading exponents of the Beaux-Arts style. They designed the Ritz Hotel, London (1903–6), as well as smaller commissions such as the interior of the Regency country house Polesden Lacey in Surrey (1906) for Mrs Ronald Greville, the daughter of the founder of a successful Scottish brewery. The Drawing Room decorated with carved and gilt panelling from a North Italian palace of *c.* 1700 provided the perfect setting to impress her aristocratic guests.

It was against a background of such historicism that designers in Belgium and France created a style without historical precedent that made new use of materials such as iron, and was directed towards the middle classes and intelligentsia rather than the very wealthy. The style is characterized by the asymmetrical whiplash line that gives a sense of dynamic movement wherever it is applied: to furniture, wallpapers, stained glass and metalwork. Although interior design had yet to emerge as a profession, the influence of the British arts and crafts movement led Continental architects and theorists to approach the planning and decorating of interiors with a respect that had traditionally been reserved for the exterior. From 1893, art nouveau architect-designers concerned themselves with all the elements of a building, from the architectural shell down to the door handles. To create a fully integrated and contemporary environment was the pivotal aim of the movement.

Art nouveau was indebted to the arts and crafts for its flowing line, simplicity in furniture design and rejection of academic models. Its formal inspiration also came from post-impressionist and symbolist painting. The threatening vortices of Van Gogh and Edvard Munch, the alluring curves of Gauguin and Aubrey Beardsley have their counterparts in the art nouveau interior. Artists and designers shared an admiration for Japanese art that manifested itself in an ubiquitous asymmetry.

Unlike the arts and crafts designers, avant-garde designers on the Continent were eager to exploit new technological advances. The progress made in iron construction during the second half of the nineteenth century is crucial for the development of the art nouveau interior. The French engineer Gustave Eiffel (1832–1923) pioneered the use of exposed-metal frameworks for buildings, exemplified by his Galerie des Machines at the Paris Exhibition of 1867. The influential French architectural theorist Eugène-Emmanuel Viollet-le-Duc (1814–1879) advocated the combination of iron and masonry in his *Entretiens sur l'Architecture* (1872), which was read by leading art nouveau designers including Victor Horta, Hector Guimard, Antoni Gaudí and the American Louis Sullivan. The early art nouveau's frank exposure of metal in the domestic interior had radical implications in the context of the traditional styles and materials used by Beaux-Arts architects.

In Belgium and Italy the style was linked with socialism. The style's Belgian originator, the architect-designer Victor Horta (1861–1947), had received a traditional academic training, and made a career designing houses for bourgeois intellectual patrons in the Ixelles suburb of Brussels. In 1896, however, he was invited to design the Brussels Maison des Peuples by members of the Parti Ouvrier Belge, the chief socialist party in Belgium, which in 1894 had achieved some measure of success by winning twenty-eight seats in parliament. Thereafter, Maisons des Peuples were built in most Belgian cities to provide meeting-places for workers' organizations. The young Horta's style was considered fitting for the new building in lacking the aristocratic overtones of the Beaux-Arts.

Horta exploited the formal possibilities of an exposed-iron frame by moulding pillars and beams into organic curves. Most successful was the double-storey auditorium at the top of the building. Acoustically the large space worked perfectly, and the winding tendrils that became a hallmark of the style were used for the metalwork banisters, beams and supporting columns.

Horta's earliest interior in the style he pioneered was the Tassel house at 6 Rue Paul-Emile Janson, Ixelles, designed for a professor of geometry, Émile Tassel, and completed in 1893. There are some restrained organic motifs in the exterior decoration, but, as with most later art nouveau buildings, the originality is in the interior. Like all Horta's designs of the period, the Tassel house plan allows free circulation throughout the principal rooms. Internal walls are reduced in number by means of cast-iron supports in the centre of the house. Horta does not disguise the metalwork infrastructure of the house but incorporates it into the design. In the hall, for example, the supporting metal column of the stair and the beams are embellished with swirling metal tendrils, and the same organic forms are painted on the wall, carried out in

1

mosaic on the floor and repeated in the metal light fitting and banister.

An indication of Horta's English sources for this style comes with the use of an English wallpaper in the dining room. This was probably an arts and crafts design by the Century Guild designer Heywood Sumner for Jeffery and Co., the company that printed William Morris's first wallpaper designs. Horta may have seen it at an exhibition in Brussels in 1872–3, or at the Paris Exposition of 1889.

A group of avant-garde artists known as Les Vingt had been formed in 1884 in Brussels to hold discussions and exhibitions with the purpose of finding a successor to French Impressionism. Important exhibitions for the creation of Belgian art nouveau included those of Gauguin's paintings in 1889 and Van Gogh's in 1890. Members of Les Vingt such as Jan Tooroop (1858–1928) and Fernand Khnopff (1858–1921) showed work in a style marked by flowing lines and flat colour areas. There is no proven link between Horta and Les Vingt, but a young progressive architect in Brussels at this time would certainly have known of their activities.

Horta designed two further Ixelles houses, for the chemist Ernest Solvay at 224 Avenue Louise (1895) and for Baron Van Eetvelde at 4 Avenue Palmerston (1897). The Hôtel Solvay, like the Tassel house, has exposed-metal structural supports and organic motifs for such items as light fittings and door handles. The Hôtel van Eetvelde has as its most important interior feature a central double-storey space around which the main staircase winds. The central area is used on the principal floor as a winter garden, and is defined by a circle of slender steel pillars that support a decorative stained-glass canopy. The same motif of vine-like branches that decorates the canopy is repeated on the iron banister and for the light fittings, which continue the organic motif with shades in the form of flower-heads. The unusual manipulation of space allows the visitor to look from the dining room, through the winter garden and into the living room.

Horta designed thirteen such Brussels houses, satisfying a taste for the exotic that may have been prompted by his clients' recent colonial contacts or travels. (It was the Belgian colonies which supplied much of the wealth for the art nouveau decoration of homes.) Horta termed these homes 'portrait houses', reflecting his belief that their design 'should not merely reflect the owner's life-style, but be his portrait'.

The most interesting of Horta's later domestic interiors is the house he designed for himself at 23–25 Rue Américaine, Ixelles, from 1898 (now the Horta Museum). The plan completely reworks

24

25

24 Victor Horta: ground floor, Winter Garden, Hôtel van Eetvelde, Ixelles, Brussels, 1897. The novel layout allows the occupants of one first-floor room to look through the Winter Garden and into the room opposite.

the conventional layout for such a townhouse. The kitchen is not located in the basement as was customary, but at ground level, and a skylight illuminates a centrally placed staircase of white Carrara marble that forms the centrepiece of the whole design, winding up through three floors. The yellow-and-white skylight has huge mirrors at either side that give an effect of infinite space. The visitor is led by this impressive stair to the upper floor of the house which contains the dining and drawing rooms.

Colour is used as the uniting feature of the dining room. The honey tones of the ash furniture, marble-faced walls, copper picture rails and painted decoration create an overall impression of simple elegance and lightness that is not found in the grander interiors of the period. The white-enamelled bricks covering the walls instead of wallpaper were an especially unusual feature. For the floor covering

25 Victor Horta: dining room of his house, Ixelles, 1898. Honey-toned ash combined with white-enamelled wallbricks create a warm, elegant and unpretentious interior. A serving hatch opens above the gas fire, with recesses at either side to keep food warm.

Horta chose, not carpeting, but wood-parquet with a border of mosaic with copper inlay, to echo the clear-cut linear motifs of the painted ironwork arch supports. Typically, Horta did not disguise these supports but made them a feature. Throughout the house, Horta's attention to detail is evident: light-fittings, door handles and towel rails have a consistent organic motif to give unity to the interior. Horta also applied organic ornament to department-store interiors, particularly A l'Innovation (1901) in Brussels and Grand Bazar (1903) in Frankfurt.

A contemporary of Horta, Paul Hankar (1859–1901), was responsible for the art nouveau design of smaller Brussels shops and houses: the Niguet Shirt Shop (1899) and his own house (1893) look solid and clumsy when compared with Horta's graceful designs. His display screens for the Ethnographical Rooms of the Brussels-Tervueren Colonial Exhibition of 1897 were topped by linear cut-outs that were based on Celtic motifs rather than on art nouveau, with broader lines and a symmetrical overall pattern. A third Belgian architect-designer, Ernest Blerot (1870–1957), used a similar style for many modest houses for Ixelles-district clients, but here too the handling of motifs is heavier and less sophisticated than Horta's. He follows a conventional plan, and the carved wood, metalwork and coloured glass used for the interior decoration lack the detail and fine craftsmanship of Horta's work.

The design theorist and propagandist Henry Van de Velde (1863–1957), author of many influential articles in French, German and Belgian periodicals and of *Die Renaissance im Modernen Kunstgewerbe* (1901), is conventionally grouped with these Belgian designers. However, at the time of Horta's buildings, Van de Velde was working within the Flemish vernacular tradition. He began work as an artist, training mainly in Paris, where he came under the influence of Van Gogh and Gauguin. Returning to Belgium he joined Les Vingt in 1888, and his paintings, graphic work and tapestries reveal these influences in their use of flat colour and rhythmic lines. He married in 1894 and decided to emulate his idol William Morris by designing a house for himself and his new bride. Indeed, Van de Velde's fiancée, Maria Sèthe, travelled to England specifically to meet Morris and buy arts and crafts wallpapers and textiles. The Villa Bloemenwerf of 1895 at Uccle near Brussels echoes earlier British models, particularly the designs of Voysey and Baillie Scott. It has a double-storey hall that acts as a focus for the interior, overlooked by various passages and rooms on the upper floor. Van de Velde designed modest, solid furniture and simple naturalistic wallpaper for his house. His intention with his first attempt at wallpaper design would seem to have been to achieve overall integration, for as he wrote: 'the three colours, amaranth-red, blue and green, were repeated in the plaster, in the grey and deep green of the gable and in the reddish roof-tiles.'

The new Belgian interior design began to influence the French as designers and shop-owners visited Brussels. The first Parisian designer to do so was Hector Guimard (1867–1942), who is best known for his metalwork for the Paris Metro stations. He had already begun to practise as an architect when, early in 1895, he went to Brussels and met Horta. This meeting and his inspection of the Tassel house inspired Guimard to rethink the interior design of a commission on which he was then working, the Castel Béranger apartment block (1895–7) at Rue La Fontaine. Although Guimard had already applied for planning permission for the apartments and could alter little of the architecture, the decorative features could be reworked in response to Horta's new style. Guimard was able to design furniture, wallpapers, carpets, mosaic floors and even door handles for the thirty-six apartments, using a sinuous, asymmetrical line. The importance Guimard attached to these designs is indicated by his publication of a luxury volume of coloured drawings, *L'Art dans l'Habitation Moderne, Le Castel Béranger* (1898). Forty-one of the sixty-five illustrations show various interiors and details of furniture and fittings.

Guimard devoted much space to the entrance hall, which is the most distinctive and exciting feature of the interior. The wrought iron and copper gate at the entrance to the hall uses all the main ingredients of art nouveau design: it is asymmetrical, the ornament is derived from natural forms, and the dynamic whiplash line is used repeatedly. The same contorted shapes appear on the green ceramic panels that line the hall, in the carpets, on the banisters and in the coloured glass. The apartments are comparatively sparsely decorated. Stylistic unity was achieved by using asymmetrical, elongated, winding forms for all the furniture and fittings. Such forms are more extreme than their Belgian counterparts, with fireplaces, settees and door-handles moulded into fluid and contorted shapes.

While they had attracted much criticism in the press for their extreme styling, the apartments were let easily and profitably. Guimard installed his studio there, and went on to use the style in other private interiors, including his own house at 122 Avenue Mozart, Paris (1909–12). The artistic synthesis achieved in these interiors, with art nouveau windows, plasterwork, furniture and light fittings, is reminiscent of the rococo interiors of eighteenth-century Paris, for example the Hôtel de Soubise. There was a rococo revival at this time in France, but the two

26 Hector Guimard: entrance hall, Castel Béranger apartments, Paris, 1895–7. The repeated whiplash line and winding tendrils on the columns reveal a recent visit to Horta in Brussels.

styles are quite distinct. They have asymmetry and playful curves in common, but where rococo merely embellishes classical proportions, art nouveau melts them away.

Horta was an important influence on Guimard, but Van de Velde was the designer who did most to propagate the new style in France and Germany. In 1895 he received two important visitors from Paris at the Villa Bloemenwerf: the art dealer Samuel Bing and the art critic Julius Meier-Graefe. Bing had previously owned a shop selling oriental goods in Paris, and on 26 December 1895 opened a shop and gallery, the 'Salon de l'Art Nouveau', in the Rue de Provence. Bing invited Van de Velde to contribute four room-settings to his shop. The designs caused a great stir in the press, with opinions both for and against, and helped to establish the 'art nouveau' style in interior design in France.

An organic style had already been developing in France with the glass and furniture of Émile Gallé (1846–1904) and the group of designers who worked with him in Nancy, which included the prominent furniture designer and manufacturer Louis Majorelle (1859–1926). Gallé was inspired by organic forms,

The Search for a New Style

27 Guimard in his studio in the Castel Béranger, c. 1903. The photograph was printed as a postcard advertising the 'Style Guimard', as Guimard termed art nouveau.

and kept a comprehensive collection of plants in the grounds of his factory, where they served as living models for his marquetry designs. Believing that all artistic inspiration should come from nature, Gallé was critical of the more contorted and exaggerated designs being shown at the turn of the century, and always used traditional forms for his own furniture, allowing art nouveau surface decoration only. Gallé was among those who exhibited at Samuel Bing's shop, the main centre of the display of art nouveau interior decoration. At exhibitions held there and at the Paris Exposition of 1900, Bing used room-settings to show the work of such important French (or French domiciled) designers as Edward Colonna, Georges de Feure and Eugène Gaillard, as well as designers from Britain and America who were searching for a new style, including Charles Rennie Mackintosh (1868–1928) and Louis Comfort Tiffany (1848–1933), who both showed work at the opening exhibition in 1895.

While the new interior design style was flourishing in France, it was also beginning to make an impact in Germany through the medium of the British arts and crafts movement and the work of Van de Velde. In 1898 Meier-Graefe commissioned furniture from Van de Velde for his own Paris showrooms, 'La Maison Moderne', established a year earlier in competition with Bing's 'Art Nouveau'. He also featured Van de Velde's work in his small-circulation magazine *Pan,* published in Germany. *Pan* had been modelled by Meier-Graefe on *The Studio* magazine, which had brought stimulating news of British arts and crafts theory and design to Germany since its foundation in 1893. The keen German interest in British interior design is exemplified in the work of Hermann Muthesius (1861–1927), an attaché at the German Embassy in London from 1895 to 1903, who made a thorough survey of English domestic architecture of the later nineteenth century, including the work of Voysey, Baillie Scott and Ashbee. His admiration for the arts and crafts and the functional design of British interiors was recorded in his influential book *Das englische Haus* (1904–5).

German art nouveau was known as *Jugendstil,* 'Young style', from a periodical, *Jugend*, founded in Munich in 1896, and the

28 Eugène Vallin: dining room, displayed at the Salon d'Automne, 1910. The organic, deeply moulded curves typify the École de Nancy, but Vallin rarely used marquetry decoration, and only occasionally incorporated carved floral motifs.

29 ABOVE Henry Van de Velde: Havana Tobacco Company cigar shop, Berlin, 1899. Sweeping curves echo Gauguin's painting and the Belgian artists of Les Vingt, as well as ubiquitous arts and crafts influence. On the walls they playfully suggest curling cigar smoke.

30 LEFT August Endell: staircase and hall, Atelier Elvira, Munich, 1897–8: *Jugendstil* at its most extreme, with dreamlike, floating marine motifs.

31 OPPOSITE Charles Rennie Mackintosh: drawing room, Hill House, Helensburgh, 1902. The gesso panel above the fire is by Mackintosh's wife Margaret Macdonald. Mackintosh's decoration combines geometrical motifs with art nouveau.

name reflects the desire of avant-garde designers to throw off historicism and create something entirely fresh for the new century. After successfully designing a rest-room for the 1897 art nouveau exhibition in Dresden, Van de Velde arrived in Berlin in 1899. The interior of François Haby's barber's shop (1900) and the Havana Tobacco Company cigar shop (1899–1900) are designed in a somewhat heavy version of art nouveau adapted to German taste. The paintwork on the walls is partly geometric, and the carved wooden shelving in the cigar shop, unlike French art nouveau, is entirely symmetrical, with thick, sweeping curves. The barber's shop design caused a great outcry in the press, for Van de Velde had decided to leave the plumbing and light-cables exposed.

29

German designers who developed *Jugendstil* included August Endell (1871–1925), whose Atelier Elvira, Munich (1897–8), has an iron staircase and light-fitting contorted into fantastic marine-inspired shapes. The light-fitting rises out of the curved newel post like a giant piece of floating seaweed. *Jugendstil* proved short-lived, and by 1901, when Endell designed the Buntes Theater, Berlin, a more controlled, geometric effect is evident, probably inspired by the work of the Glasgow School (page 54), which was making an impact in Europe through *The Studio* from 1897 onwards.

30

32 Antoni Gaudí: dining room, Casa Batlló, Barcelona, 1904–6. Window frames, doors and furniture melt into the exuberant curves of Gaudí's *arte moderno*.

In Russia, a revival of national folk crafts had gained momentum during the 1870s, and their styles mingled with the influence of European symbolism and French art nouveau. Moscow was the centre of the *stil moderne* in Russia, and Fedor Shekhtel (1859–1926) united the three influences in designing the Ryabushinsky house (1900) and the Derozhinskaia house (1901). His upholstery fabric for armchairs is based on the rhythmical use of line seen at this time in the paintings of Mikhail Vrubel (1856–1910), an artist, theatrical designer and craftsman who had worked at the artists' colony established by Princess Tenisheva on her estate of Talashkino, and at the similar colony at Abramtsevo. Vrubel provided ceramic wall-decoration and mural paintings for the Ryabushinsky house. In the library of the house, designed for the singer Derozhinskaia, Shekhtel uses the sinuous line of art nouveau to decorate the wooden doors and built-in seating.

In Spain and Italy as in Russia, art nouveau was used as an expression of new national and political aspirations. The cradle of *arte moderno* (as the style was known in Spain) was the Catalan capital of Barcelona, then attempting to break free from Spanish domination. The most prominent architect-designer in the style was Antoni Gaudí (1852–1926), who expressed his religious beliefs and fervent nationalism through his designs for apartment blocks and churches. His inspiration came partly from organic sources, by way of Viollet-le-Duc, partly from the arts and crafts movement via *The Studio,* and partly from his own desire to design without historical reference. He designed complete interiors with organic or flowing, lava-like forms. The commission for the Casa Batlló (1904–6) was to reface and refurbish an apartment block. The interiors have undulating ceilings and strangely curved window- and door-frames, and contain biomorphic furniture designed by Gaudí himself and carved in solid oak.

The *Stile Liberty,* as it was known in Italy because of the influence of the London store of that name, was associated with the new wave of Italian mild socialism, democracy, and the entry of Italy into the international arena as a manufacturing nation. The International Exhibition of Decorative Art held in Turin in 1902 was planned to assist the regeneration of the once-great Italian city, and the number of countries and exhibitors who participated exceeded the organizers' expectations. The exhibition provided the most comprehensive international overview of art nouveau. The many interiors on view included examples by Van de Velde, Horta and Guimard. The site and pavilions were designed by the leading Italian art nouveau architect, Raimondo D'Aronco (1857–1932), whose Central Rotunda with its rich and detailed decoration was intended as a monument to the movement. The interior plasterwork was painted with highly stylized flowers and abstract grids. Italian designers whose international careers were promoted by the exhibition included Carlo Bugatti, a member of the famous car-designing family, whose exotic interiors and furniture were heavily indebted to African sources, and who used unusual materials such as vellum and pewter inlay. At the Turin Exhibition he showed a suite of rooms, the most extreme of which was the Camera de Bovolo (Snail Room) with furniture based on the snail-shell spiral.

The *stile Liberty* continued to flourish in Italy after 1902 when elsewhere art nouveau had passed its peak. Giuseppe Sommaruga (1867–1917) used it for commissions such as the Palazzo Castiglioni (1903) in Milan, as did Giovanni Michelazzi for his Villino Lampredi (1908–12) in Florence.

The work of American art nouveau designers shown at the 1902 Turin Exhibition included that of Louis Comfort Tiffany, whose exotic glassware was inspired by Gallé and Bing. American architect-designers had also been working

33 Carlo Bugatti: Snail Room, Turin Exhibition, 1902. Curved fitted seating terminates in a circular cupboard, and separate chairs and table continue the snail-shell motif.

against the empty historicism of the Beaux-Arts towards the creation of a new style. The movement was led by the architect-designer Louis Sullivan (1856–1924), who succeeded in finding appropriate ornament for innovative architectural structure. After a brief architectural training, partly at the École des Beaux-Arts, in 1881 Sullivan went into partnership with the engineer Dankmar Adler (1844–1900) in Chicago. The firm's first major commission came with the Auditorium Building, constructed 1887–90, and at the time the city's largest building.

34

The Auditorium is noteworthy in the history of interior design because it is here that electric light was used for the first time as a design feature. The impressive 'Golden Arches' that span its theatre interior are decorated in an eclectic style, with luscious gilded plant-forms picked out with clear electric light bulbs. Although non-structural, the arches were used to conceal ventilation ducts and improve the acoustics. The effectiveness of the overall colour scheme of gold and ivory and the use of new technology ensured that the fame of the theatre interior spread worldwide, and it was regarded by some critics as the modern successor to the Paris Opéra. Sullivan justified his decorative schemes by reference to a number of theories, and took his inspiration from sources as varied as oriental art, Ruskin and Darwinism, believing that decoration should relate to natural forms. Like art nouveau architect-designers in Europe, Sullivan developed a new language of ornament to suit new building types such as the department store.

It was in the Chicago offices of Adler and Sullivan that Frank Lloyd Wright (1867–1959) learned the foundations of architectural design and theory, and it was he who succeeded in establishing a distinctive American style for domestic and commercial interiors. During the first years of the century Wright shared the concern of his European counterparts for the integrated interior and their disdain for historical precedent. Much of Wright's early career as an independent designer was devoted to houses in and around Chicago, described as 'prairie houses' because of their proximity to and sympathy with the huge, flat expanses of land in the Midwest. The houses are usually planned around a central core provided by a brick or stone fireplace, reminiscent in this of American seventeenth-century Colonial houses. Interiors such as those of the Martin House (1904–6) at Buffalo and the Robie House (1909) in Chicago provide a flowing, integrated space, with the fireplace as the symbolic heart. Wright's responsibility for the entire look of the interior, from architecture to furniture to textiles, is well illustrated by the living room of the Francis W. Little House (1912–14), Wayzata, Minnesota (now installed in the American

34 Louis Sullivan with Dankmar Adler: theatre of the Auditorium Building, Chicago, 1887–90. The influences of art nouveau and the Beaux-Arts style combine to brilliant effect in the famous 'Golden Arches'.

35 Frank Lloyd Wright: Francis W. Little House, Wayzata, Minnesota, 1912–14. A protean designer, Wright adapted a design of horizontals and verticals and the use of natural materials to create a uniquely American style of expression.

Wing of the Metropolitan Museum of Art, New York). The entire decoration is based on horizontals and verticals, from the square electroglazed skylights to the box-like upholstered chair that makes few concessions to the human form. The interior is further unified by Wright's use of oak treated only with blond wax for both the furniture and fixtures such as wall-lamps.

Wright's designs for commercial buildings of this period include the Larkin Administration Building, Buffalo (1904), where the most striking feature of the interior is a five-storey skylit atrium with all its services concealed in corner pillars. The interior is sparse, faced with cream-coloured brick. Here again Wright designed the furniture, including early examples of metal chairs and desks.

The Turin Exhibition of 1902 marked the beginning of the decline of art nouveau as an avant-garde movement. Demand for the style reached saturation point very quickly. During the years leading up to the First World War, the avant-garde interior

36 Wright's Larkin Administration Building, Buffalo, New York, 1904. An early example of the central atrium for office use. In contrast with Wright's private houses, the building looks entirely inwards, and it was one of the earliest offices to be equipped with climate control.

The Search for a New Style

became simpler and more geometric. This trend is already evident in Wright's interiors, and can be observed in the work of designers in Britain and Austria.

The art nouveau style never found favour in Britain, and was criticized by leading designers there for its exoticism and femininity. This was an opinion shared by the Glasgow School, centred loosely around the Glasgow School of Art at the turn of the century. It never identified itself with art nouveau, but only with the search for a new style. George Walton (1867–1933) was typical in taking his inspiration from Voysey and the traditional Scottish interior with its inglenook, as well as from Celtic sources. He developed a successful interior-design business, first in Glasgow and then London, and worked extensively for George Davison, head of European sales for Kodak, designing many of their showrooms in the Glasgow Style. Walton's work was well known throughout Europe, but he continued to work within a simplified, vernacular tradition and was not deeply affected by developments on the Continent.

The same could not be said of his contemporary Charles Rennie Mackintosh, arguably the most original architect-

37 George Walton: Kodak shop, London, 1900. Walton's high-backed settees and geometrical stencilled decoration typify the Celtic influence and the style of the Glasgow School.

designer working during the period. After studying at the Glasgow School of Art, Mackintosh was apprenticed to the academic architect, John Hutchinson. In 1890 he travelled to France and Italy, and on his return to Glasgow worked with his future wife Margaret Macdonald, her sister Frances and her future husband, Herbert McNair. Known as The Four, they exhibited their symbolist-inspired graphic work at Samuel Bing's showroom in Paris during 1895.

Mackintosh is acclaimed today first as an architect and second as a furniture designer, but it was as a designer of interiors that he was best known during his lifetime. Key commissions came from the eccentric Catherine Cranston, a hotelier's daughter who developed the tearoom business in Glasgow for the city's burgeoning nouveau-riche clientele. Mackintosh was commissioned by George Walton to redesign the furniture and fittings for the Crown Lunch and Tea Rooms in 1896, and later in the same year, in turn commissioned Walton to design the furniture for the Buchanan Street Tea Rooms. Both these early designs were within the arts and crafts tradition of Lethaby and Voysey, with the use of heart-shaped motifs and unpolished ash furniture. Mackintosh's next design for Cranston in 1900, at the Ingram Street Tea Room, was entirely his own and used the white-painted furniture that had become a feature of his most recent designs, including that of his own modest house at 120 Mains Street, Glasgow (1900), which are now preserved by the University of Glasgow.

A hallmark of these interiors was the use of bold contrasts between light and dark. In Mains Street Mackintosh created an intimate atmosphere in his dining room with the sombre brown of the walls, which were covered with coarse wrapping-paper. The stained-oak chairs have 135 cm (53 inch) high backs, when measured from the floor, and so help to subdivide the space of the room when the diners are seated, adding to the sense of intimacy. The darkness of the furniture and walls is set off by white paint above the picture rail and on the ceiling.

In the drawing room Mackintosh created an equally dramatic effect with white for the wall and floor coverings as well as for the majority of the furniture. He created a light and spacious living area, diffusing natural daylight with muslin stretched over the windows. The desk, bookcase and fireplace are all white-enamel-painted to ensure that no detail of joints or grain of the wood detracted from the sculptural effect. The furniture was also very carefully placed, revealing Mackintosh's debt to Japanese house-design. To contemporary taste at the turn of the century such an interior appeared sparse, and the decoration mean.

38–40 Charles Rennie
Mackintosh: (above)
sitting room, Mains
Street, Glasgow, 1900;
(left) Derngate, guest
bedroom, 1919; (opposite)
Hill House, Helensburgh,
1902. Light and clear
design of Japanese
and organic inspiration
(Mains Street) yields first
to rectangular motifs
(Hill House), and finally
to strongly geometric
design (Derngate),
reflecting the contacts
between Mackintosh
and the designers of
the Vienna Secession
and Werkstätte.

Even when working on a complete building, Mackintosh began his design from the inside out, defining the particular requirements of the clients before considering the outside appearance. The procedure is well documented in the design of Hill House, Helensburgh (1902), for the publisher Walter Blackie and his family, where Mackintosh spent much time discovering how the family lived before embarking on his designs. Mackintosh's planning of Hill House was also based on his competition entry for 'the House of an Art Lover' of 1901, in which he came second to Baillie Scott (largely because he failed to comply with the rules, which stipulated interior perspectives). Like the House of an Art Lover, Hill House had a carefully planned interior, where the children's nursery was placed as far away as possible from the parents' living and sleeping areas.

40   At Hill House as in other projects, the dining room was decorated in dark tones, on this occasion with wood panelling. In the drawing room Mackintosh succeeded in dividing the limited space into smaller zones for different activities. There is an area by the piano for musical evenings, seats around the fire for reading and conversation, and a bay window with a fitted seat and shelving, for contemplation of the view. The walls are

decorated with a stencilled design of pink roses on a formalized blue trellis pattern. The floral inspiration was important for Mackintosh, and can be seen again in the columns at either side of the window seat. White predominates. As in his own house, it made a clean, uncluttered interior.

The main bedroom makes a similar effect with white-painted furniture and highlights of rose-coloured glass, but Mackintosh now began to introduce more geometrical elements. The tiny panes of coloured glass in the doors and window-shutters are square, and the shape of the furniture is also more box-like.

His final commission for Miss Cranston was 'Willow Teas' (1904) in the fashionable shopping area of Sauchiehall Street, Glasgow. In the Room De Luxe ladies could look out upon the street through leaded windows that included mirror-glass. Mirror-glass was used for the surrounding wall-frieze and enhanced the atmosphere of luxury. The characteristic high-backed chairs are painted an unfamiliar silver.

41 Mackintosh's last great interior in the city was the Library of the Glasgow School of Art, one of the most spectacular of the period. He had won the competition to design the School in 1896; part of his design was built, opening in 1899, and the Library was added in 1907–9, at the same time as the West Wing. The bookshop over the ground floor of the Library building is suspended on steel stirrups from the beams that support the floor above, allowing a freer use of ground-floor space, which with its exposed timber supports and carefully planned lighting appears immensely greater than its actual 11 metres (36 feet) square.

Mackintosh left Glasgow in 1914 as interest in his work declined, probably intending to go to Vienna where appreciation of his work was greater. On the outbreak of the First World War he settled first in Walberswick, Suffolk, and then in Chelsea, London. He found his last patron in the model-engineering manufacturer and early member of the Design and Industries Association, W.J. Bassett-Lowke, who commissioned him to

39 design the interior of his house at 78 Derngate, Northampton, in 1916. Because of his engineering background and European contacts, Bassett-Lowke wanted an impressive but functional design. Mackintosh responded with a black entrance hall with a stencilled band of black and white squares, and above it a painted frieze composed of yellow, grey, vermilion, blue, green and purple triangles. The geometrical theme was repeated in furniture with lattice squares.

Mackintosh's move from organically inspired geometrical motifs had begun at Hill House in 1902, and was furthered by his contacts with Viennese designers after he had exhibited

41 Charles Rennie Mackintosh: Library, Glasgow School of Art, 1907–9.
The double-storey height of the small room is emphasized by vertical
columns and electric lights suspended on long chains.

The Search for a New Style

Vienna in 1900. He was recalled by Bassett-Lowke in 1919 to design the guest bedroom at Derngate, the last and perhaps the most startling interior of his short career. The room was painted white except for the wall behind the two beds and the ceiling directly above them, which is papered with black-and-white stripes trimmed with ultramarine ribbon. All the fabrics in the room were integrated into the scheme, with printed stripes and appliqué squares. The furniture was not overpowered in this dazzling ensemble: the light oak was painted with a black stripe and blue squares. The combination of strong colours and geometrical details, particularly lines of small squares, reveals the mutual influence of Mackintosh and the designers of the Vienna Secession.

Although Mackintosh was largely ignored in Britain (the Derngate interiors were illustrated in *Ideal Home* in 1920 without mention of his name), he had attracted admiration throughout the rest of Europe. A simpler style in reaction to

42 Otto Wagner: main counter hall, Austrian Post Office Savings Bank, Vienna, 1904–6. Wagner planned the plain and clear interior in great detail, constructing a model 'counter' in 1905. The tidy cube-shaped desks and stools are dark-stained beechwood.

art nouveau was beginning to emerge in Germany and Austria, where designers associated with the Vienna Secession, founded in 1897, and the Wiener Werkstätte, founded in 1903, admired the starkness of Mackintosh's designs. His work had been publicized in articles in *The Studio* written by Gleeson White in 1897, and in illustrations in the periodical *Dekorative Kunst* in the following year and in various later avant-garde periodicals. Mackintosh took part in the 1900 Secession Exhibition in Vienna, showing a tea room.

The Vienna Secession was a breakaway exhibition society for Austrian and other European avant-garde painters and architects who were dissatisfied with the dominance of the Academy of Fine Arts. One of its principal aims was to dissolve existing barriers between art and design. This was to be accomplished by the arts and crafts method of the fine artist or architect applying his superior taste and vision to design concerns. It is indicative that one of the founder-members of the Secession, Josef Hoffmann (1870–1956), is referred to in *The Studio* as 'Architect *and* Decorator'.

The Secession elevated the status of design by giving it a prominent role in exhibitions. The first Secession exhibition of 1898 showed paintings by the Belgian symbolist artist Fernand Khnopff, lithographs by Whistler, works by one of the founder-members, the painter Gustav Klimt, and Walter Crane's book illustrations, alongside designs for wallpaper and stained glass. Hoffmann created the *Ver Sacrum* room especially for the exhibition (named after the magazine of the Secession, founded in 1898). The room itself and the furniture were both simple. Whereas in art nouveau the unifying visual element was the taut whiplash line, here the dominant motif was the vertical. The chair-backs, table-legs, cabinet-fronts and door frames were all in the form of three parallel strips of wood. The starkness of the room was increased by plain wall- and floor-coverings and simple curtains at the window.

So great was the financial success of the exhibition that the Secession was able to build its own exhibition hall in the same year. The founder-member Joseph Maria Olbrich (1867–1908) combined geometrical design and motifs with a huge dome of golden intertwined laurel branches. The interior is designed for maximum flexibility of use.

The second Secession exhibition showed architectural drawings by Otto Wagner (1841–1918), the father of the Viennese avant-garde, whose liberal teaching methods had encouraged Hoffmann and Olbrich. His design for the Post Office Savings Bank in Vienna (1904–6) includes one of the clearest and most functional interiors of the early twentieth century. The main

42

43 Josef Hoffmann and Koloman Moser: main hall, Purkersdorf Sanatorium, 1904–5. Chairs, floor and wall design emphasize the theme of the square.

hall has a glass barrel-vaulted roof, plain metal pillars, and aluminium hot-air-blowers that punctuate the wall-space at regular intervals. Such a plain interior was the antithesis of the Revivalist splendour prevailing in Vienna, particularly with the Ringstrasse completed in 1888. Simple room settings formed a major part of Secession exhibitions until the group dissolved in 1905.

The success of the Secession and the ideals of the British arts and crafts movement inspired Hoffmann and the designer Koloman Moser (1868–1918) to found the Wiener Werkstätte in 1903 as a modest crafts workshop. Like the arts and crafts movement, Hoffmann and Moser were opposed to the methods of mass production, and aimed to use only materials and skills of the highest quality. This failure to come to terms with twentieth-century means of production led the Werkstätte to produce only precious objects for wealthy customers.

The Werkstätte had an architect's office for the coordination of building and interior design, and the first major commission was for a sanatorium at Purkersdorf (1904–5). Hoffmann was responsible for the whole design, to the last detail, of this early iron and concrete building, including the furnishings, decorations and appliances that were made in the Werkstätte studios. As with the *Ver Sacrum* room, the interior design is restrained and functional. It is based entirely on horizontals and verticals: the entrance-hall floor tiles form a pattern of

43

44-5 Josef Hoffmann and the Wiener Werkstätte: dining room and central hall, Palais Stoclet, Brussels, 1905–11. A 'total artwork' executed for a wealthy patron, and demonstrating that design based on rectangles was just as appropriate for luxurious furnishings as for functional interiors.

The Search for a New Style

squares, the backs and sides of chairs are constructed of a square framing seven vertical slats, and even Hoffmann's designs for smaller objects such as a silver tea service and trays are based on the square.

44-5 The Werkstätte's most significant commission, the Palais Stoclet in the Avenue de Tervueren, Brussels (1905–11), represented the successful collaboration of architect-designers, craftsworkers and fine artists. Here the Werkstätte had no need to compromise the principle of using the finest materials and best workmanship; the palatial residence was designed for a millionaire banker, Adolphe Stoclet, who put no limit on expenditure. Hoffmann and the Werkstätte designed the building, the garden, the interior and all the fittings, down to the cutlery. It was the ultimate *Gesamtkunstwerk* or 'total work of art'. The central hall rising through two storeys had columns and walls faced with yellow and brown marble, parquet flooring, and low-backed easy chairs and sofas covered in chamois. The narrow dining room is faced with marble. Above its continuous sideboards running the length of the room are art nouveau frieze panels by Gustav Klimt. The mosaic of silver, enamel, coral and semi-precious stones depicts formalized figures and scroll-like trees-of-life.

In common with most interior design described in this chapter, the Palais Stoclet was a unique commission. Architect-designers had yet to come to terms with the challenge of mass production and attempted to continue in a pre-industrial age. As the Austrian correspondent of *The Studio* explained: 'The future of modern art rests with the middle class, but they need educating. They are worth educating too; nothing proves this here in Vienna more than the rush for the modern during the past five or six years. But it behoves those who cater for this class to be very careful only to produce really good things, perfect in design and workmanship. If the public is taught how to distinguish true art from the many varieties of false, it will appreciate each at its proper value. True, it costs more to produce superior articles, but the expense is only an initial one, for in this, as in other things, in the long run good articles are cheaper – and, moreover, they often come to have an intrinsic worth of their own.' Modern movement designers were to address the challenge of mass taste with varying degrees of success during the next avant-garde phase of interior design.

Chapter 3
The Modern Movement

Inspired by a new machine aesthetic, the modern movement stripped away unnecessary ornament from the interior. Mass production was now established as the means of manufacturing consumer goods, and modern movement theorists were inspired by the concepts of rationalization and standardization. New materials and building techniques were to be used to create a lighter, more spacious and functional environment. The early modern designers hoped to change society for the better with the creation of a healthier and more democratic type of design for all.

The first designer categorically to reject the need for ornament in interior design was the Austrian architect Adolf Loos (1870–1933). Loos's three years spent in America from 1893 to 1896 may explain his total aversion to the florid excesses of art nouveau and the 'precious' interiors of the Wiener Werkstätte. During his time in America he became familiar with the work of Louis Sullivan and Frank Lloyd Wright, and he missed the formative years of art nouveau in Europe. This, together with an admiration for the British arts and crafts movement, led Loos to reject ornamentation as degenerate. His best-known critical essay, 'Ornament and Crime', first published in the liberal *Neue Freie Presse* in January 1908, argued that the urge to decorate surfaces was primitive, and instanced a link between tattoos and modern criminals and the case of graffiti on lavatory walls as evidence. While such polemic was obviously not to be taken too seriously, Loos did succeed in challenging the belief of the art nouveau designers that all surfaces should be decorated. His writing and interior design inspired the generation of architects that went on to create the modern movement.

46 LEFT Adolf Loos: living room, Moller House, near Vienna, 1928. Four steps separate the two levels.
47 BELOW Adolf Loos: American Bar, Kärntnerstrasse, Vienna, 1907. Mirrors provide recession and the play of rectangles.

Loos worked as an interior designer in pre-war Vienna on a variety of domestic and public commissions. His designs for the Leopold Langer Flat of 1901, his own flat of *c.* 1903 and the Steiner House of 1910 reveal his skill in handling interior spaces. Exposed beams and modest furniture create a comfortable rather than ostentatious interior. Loos used built-in furniture whenever possible as part of his *Raumplan,* or plan of volumes. This involved the complex ordering of internal space, culminating in the split-level areas of the Moller House of 1928 in Vienna and the Müller House of 1930 near Prague. The horizontal and vertical elements of the living room of the Moller House are emphasized by black ceiling beams and black wooden strips outlining the door frame, shelving and window frame, to give an overall effect of the play of rectangular planes. Loos's expert handling of space is also demonstrated in public commissions such as the American Bar in the Kärntnerstrasse, Vienna, of 1907. Here the coffered yellow marble ceiling and plain green marble piers are reflected in mirrors that are set above the high mahogany wainscotting to give the impression of greater space in a room measuring only 3.5 by 7 metres (11½ by 23 feet). Because of the height of the mirrors the customer is not reflected, and the illusion of depth is enhanced.

Although feted by the modern movement ('Ornament and Crime' was reprinted in Le Corbusier's *L'Esprit Nouveau* in 1920), Loos never joined its ranks. He acted as a catalyst for the sweeping away of surface decoration, but his work was rooted in the nineteenth century and not concerned with the problems of mass production. Peter Behrens (1868–1940) was another architect of Loos's generation to inspire the modern movement. Behrens's work for AEG, the German general electrical company, forged new links between art and industry. Behrens gave the company's graphics, industrial design and factories a clean-lined, modern look and made full use of newly developed materials. The AEG Turbine Factory of 1909–10 in Berlin was constructed of poured concrete and exposed steel. No attempt was made by Behrens to disguise the structure with applied ornament.

Behrens's work for AEG was admired by fellow members of the Deutscher Werkbund, a crucial organization for the coming to terms with the age of mechanization. Founded in 1907 in Munich with the support of Hermann Muthesius and Henry Van de Velde, it aimed to improve German design by bringing manufacturers and artists together. By 1910 it had more than seven hundred members, of whom roughly half were industrialists and half artists. Rather than ignoring mass production, the Werkbund attempted to raise design standards for industry with a campaign featuring approved products in yearbooks and public propaganda. Designers involved with the Werkbund attempted to apply the new aesthetic of functionalism to the interior. Karl Schmidt was a founder member of the Werkbund and director of a furniture manufacturers, the Deutsche Werkstätten. With the help of the Werkbund designer Richard Riemerschmid (1868–1957) the firm set up a new factory for the mass production of standard furniture and prefabricated houses. The improvement of mass housing was to be one of the Werkbund's concerns.

While the Werkbund paved the way for a new aesthetic for mass-produced design, from the first there was a conflict of view between the business and artistic sections. This came to a head at the Werkbund Conference of 1914 when Muthesius proposed that design should be standardized and consist of a limited number of 'type-forms', a rationalization which would also benefit the German economy. Van de Velde argued against the reform, protesting that individual artistic inspiration would be crushed. Van de Velde won the majority support of the Werkbund, indicating the strength of fine art values among its members.

Walter Gropius (1883–1969) led the debate on the side of Van de Velde. He was convinced of the importance of individual creativity and artistic integrity while supporting a modernist aesthetic. His compartment for a Mitropa sleeping-car of c. 1914 shows a functional use of limited space, and his design for a shoe-last factory at Alfeld-an-der-Leine for Fagus of 1910–11 (with Adolf Meyer) was a prototype for the modern movement. The influence of Behrens, in whose offices Gropius had worked in 1907–10, can be seen in the monumental simplicity of the building. Its most striking feature is the staircase that runs up one corner, almost completely exposed by huge windows. Gropius made a virtue of new construction techniques. His design for a model factory at the Werkbund's Cologne Exhibition of 1914 boldly displays the spiral staircase in a wraparound glass tower.

Gropius's adventurous designs were noticed by Van de Velde, who proposed him as new director of the Weimar Kunstgewerbeschule, later to become the Bauhaus in Weimar. Gropius was appointed director after the war, and the new Bauhaus was established in 1919. The school aimed to teach the arts and crafts in tandem and to bridge the ever-widening gulf between art and industry. The Bauhaus was never to achieve its second aim; it functioned chiefly as a centre for fine art experiment and crafts production, rather than for design for

48 Richard Riemerschmid: bed-sitting-room, 1907. An economical design for the Deutsche Werkstätten, Hellerau.

industry. It was important as an international meeting-place for the development of the modern movement style.

At first the emphasis of the school was expressionist. The first Manifesto of 1919 had an expressionist woodcut by Lyonel Feininger on its cover. Expressionist painting had flourished in Germany before the war and then inspired design with an emphasis on exaggerated forms and the fantastic. It had been seen at the 1914 Werkbund Exhibition with Bruno Taut's Glass Pavilion, inspired by the mystical writer Paul Scheerbart and constructed almost entirely of glass bricks. Erich Mendelsohn's Einstein Tower at Potsdam (1919–20) and Hans Poelzig's interior of the Grosse Schauspielhaus, Berlin (1919), are further examples of this fantasy style. Poelzig used huge stalactite forms in the auditorium, built for an audience of five thousand, to create a strange and mystical atmosphere. The movement was short-lived, and was superseded by modernism as designers like Poelzig began to design in a more functional way.

The school's first commission was for the Sommerfeld House in Berlin in 1921. Designed by Gropius and Meyer with the collaboration of the students, this was built of timber and was a homage to the craft aesthetic of hand-working skills. The school lost its mystical and crafts emphasis during the 1920s with the arrival of new staff who imparted the experimentation of the international avant-garde.

No less important was the impact of De Stijl, a group founded during 1917 in neutral Holland around a small-circulation

49

49 Hans Poelzig: Grosse Schauspielhaus, Berlin, 1919. Expressionist fantasy at its zenith.

magazine of the same name. Inspired by the Neoplatonic philosophy of the Theosophists, the painter Piet Mondrian, painter, designer and theorist Theo van Doesburg and designer Gerrit Rietveld created a new aesthetic. Using only primary colours with black, grey and white, the movement attempted to create the ultimate design object which would reflect the universality and perfection of simple geometric forms. With the same purpose the De Stijl designers restricted themselves to horizontal and vertical planes wherever possible. Rietveld's Red/Blue chair of 1918 was one of the first expressions of this new aesthetic. Constructed from sheets of painted plywood simply screwed together, this seemed to represent the ultimate rethinking of a basic object. Rietveld was able to apply the aesthetic theories of De Stijl to a full-scale project in 1924 when he was commissioned to design the Schröder House in Utrecht with the owner Mrs Truus Schröder. The small suburban house is the supreme example of the De Stijl aesthetic applied to an interior.

50

The emphasis on horizontals and verticals and the restricted colour scheme give a visual unity to the exterior and interior of the house. Rietveld was inspired by Japanese house design, and by the work of Frank Lloyd Wright, whose Wasmuth publications of 1910 and 1911 containing his lecture 'The Art and Craft of the Machine', as well as plans and photographs of his work, were available to Rietveld in Holland. Both Wright's living room for the Francis Little House and Rietveld's interior repeat the motif of horizontal and vertical bars. Rietveld designed the whole building and all the fittings and fixtures throughout. The upper floor was designed to be flexible, with the rooms arranged around a stairwell, and sliding partitions to close off working/sleeping rooms, or, if left open, to allow free circulation throughout the whole floor. This exciting use of space was described in 1924 in Van Doesburg's 'Sixteen Points of a Plastic Architecture', where he writes of De Stijl theory: 'The new architecture is *anti-cubic,* that is to say, it does not try to freeze the different functional spacecells in one closed cube. Rather it throws the functional space cells (as well as overhanging planes, balcony, volumes etc.) centrifugally from the core.'

50 Gerrit Rietveld: living room, Schröder House, Utrecht, 1924. Fluid internal space encircling a central stairwell and generous fenestration reduce boundaries to a minimum. The construction of the Red/Blue Chair, 1918, is clearly expressed by the unusual joints, with the various members extending beyond their points of contact. Note the divisions on the floor, which show where sliding partitions can be used to separate living and sleeping areas.

De Stijl theories of design reached the Bauhaus when Van Doesburg (1883–1931) came to Weimar in 1921–3 and set up an unofficial course for Bauhaus students in competition with the still mystical and crafts-oriented official curriculum.

A second avant-garde movement that was to affect the direction of the Bauhaus was Constructivism. After the October Revolution of 1917 Russian avant-garde artists set out to meet the needs of the proletariat with a more material-based art and design. Vladimir Tatlin, Alexander Rodchenko, Varvara Stepanova and El Lissitsky were among those who had been fine artists before 1917, but now regarded this role as self-indulgent and superficial. They therefore set out to work at the service of the Revolution, involved with the art schools

51 Félix Del Marle: furniture, Dresden, 1926. De Stijl design by a French exponent, described by the De Stijl painter Piet Mondrian as 'the best application of neo-plasticism'.

and later designing practical items such as workers' clothing. A Soviet art exhibition was organized by El Lissitzky in Berlin in 1922, and his *Vesch* ('Object') magazine brought the message of Russian constructivism to Germany.

Radical influences such as these began to make an impact on the Bauhaus in the early 1920s. Gropius made changes in the teaching staff, taking on Wassily Kandinsky (1866–1944), the Russian pioneer of abstract painting, to run the murals workshop and László Moholy-Nagy (1895–1946), the Hungarian Constructivist, experimental painter and photographer, to run the Basic Course. The change of emphasis from crafts to modern design was seen publicly at the first full-scale exhibition of Bauhaus work in 1923. Staged to coincide with the annual Deutscher Werkbund conference held that year at Weimar, the exhibition was a huge success. The school's new approach was nowhere more visible than in a specially designed house, named for the street in which it was built, the 'Haus am Horn'. Designed by George Muche with technical advice from Adolf Meyer (1881–1929), it was constructed of steel and concrete. The plan of the house was based on a simple square, with the main living area in the centre, lit by windows in a small upper storey. The emphasis was on function, with each space having a clearly defined purpose to ensure maximum efficiency. The Bauhaus designed and made all the simple, functional fittings and furniture. The kitchen by a student, Marcel Breuer (1902–1981), is an early example of rational domestic design. It has fitted cupboards, a continuous work surface, and uniform storage jars that were already in production.

The exhibition established the Bauhaus's reputation as a leading force in the creation of a new functional aesthetic. This leadership was consolidated in 1925 when the school was forced to move from Weimar to the industrial town of Dessau, and Gropius was responsible for the design of new accommodation for the school, as well as living quarters for the students and staff. The main site consisted of connected ferro-concrete rectangular blocks for the teaching, administration and student accommodation areas. This was the first example of a large-scale public building in the modern movement style. Gropius used flat roofs throughout, and a huge glass curtain-wall for the four-storey workshop block to supply high levels of light for the studios. Technical virtuosity is celebrated in the pulley system used to open ten windows simultaneously. The Bauhaus workshops were entirely responsible for the design of the interior. The angular metal theatre lighting was designed by Moholy-Nagy and tubular metal seating by Marcel Breuer, the former student, now Bauhaus lecturer.

52 ABOVE LEFT View into the Bauhaus 'Haus am Horn', an experimental house built in a street near the school for the 1923 exhibition.
53 ABOVE RIGHT Marcel Breuer: kitchen, 1923. One of the earliest examples of a fitted kitchen with matching storage jars, designed for the first full-scale exhibition held by the Bauhaus.

Teaching-staff accommodation was located near the main site. Gropius designed a detached house for himself as Director and three pairs of semi-detached residences for other staff. Like the 'Haus am Horn', these quarters were designed strictly with function in mind. Apparently uncomfortable to live in, they were sparsely furnished and decorated with very little colour. This economic approach was best suited to bathrooms and kitchens: the kitchen in Gropius's own house is a model of efficiency and was equipped with all the latest gadgets, such as a washing machine and eye-level oven.

The move to Dessau signalled a mature phase of experimental design at the Bauhaus. Most successful of the prototypes now produced by the Bauhaus workshops were the lamp designs by students such as Marianne Brandt, K.J. Jucker and Wilhelm Wagenfeld, which were manufactured throughout the late 1920s and 1930s. The lamps were marketed as being robust, functional and stylishly modern. More commercially successful but less avant-garde were the patterned and textured wallpaper

55

designs for the firm of Rasch of Bramsche, who began production in 1930. The best-known Bauhaus products are the chairs, now regarded as icons of the modern movement. Breuer's tubular-steel chairs, notably the 'Wassily' chair designed for Kandinsky's staff house in 1925, were adapted for manufacture by Standard-Möbel. However, the materials and process used were costly, and so this range was far more expensive than the simple bentwood furniture being mass produced by the Austrian firm of Thonet Brothers. Bauhaus design was machine-inspired, and its products were designed to look as if they had been manufactured by a factory for the mass market, whereas in reality their style and cost were more likely to destine them for the fashionable middle-class interior.

In 1928 Walter Gropius resigned as Director and was replaced by the radical architect Hannes Meyer (1889–1954), who believed that the Bauhaus had become too insular and needed to make more contact with the outside world. It was during Meyer's régime that profitable links with industry were made, most notably with Rasch. He replaced the metalwork and cabinet-making workshops with a new interior design department, responsible for furniture and utensils, and the architectural department became supreme. Twelve Bauhaus students were involved in the design of mass housing at Törten, a suburb of

54 Bauhaus Theatre, Dessau, 1926. Metal and canvas seating by Marcel Breuer and angled metal light fittings by Moholy-Nagy.

55 ABOVE Walter Gropius: kitchen for the Director's house, designed after the Bauhaus had moved to Dessau, 1926. Note the latest gadgets such as an eye-level oven.
56 LEFT The Director's office, Bauhaus, Dessau, 1926. The ceiling light is by Moholy-Nagy, inspired by De Stijl. The armchair is by Gropius. The wall-hanging and the rug are by the Bauhaus Weaving workshop. Though 'decoration' was alien to the modern movement conception of functional interior design, the teaching of colour theory by the painters Klee and Kandinsky and the activities of the Weaving workshop ensured that colour and pattern retained a role.

Dessau. Meyer's Communist sympathies made him unpopular with the Dessau officials and public, and in 1930 he was forced to resign. He was replaced by the far more conservative German architect Ludwig Mies van der Rohe (1886–1969).

Mies was an unpopular choice among the students, whose interests, cultivated by Meyer, lay in the direction of mass housing and the radical possibilities of modern design. German designers elsewhere had been experimenting with such concepts. The 'Frankfurt kitchen' which had been designed by Grete Schütte-Lihotzky for the Frankfurt city architect Ernst May in 1926 was one such example. Because of a housing crisis in the city May and his team had had to design functional, cheap dwellings to accommodate the maximum number of people. Since the dwellings were small, special standardized furniture was designed to make the optimum use of space with built-in units. Designers were influenced by space-saving galleys on ships and trains, and by books on efficient household management such as Christine Frederick's *The New Housekeeping,* published in New York in 1913 and in Berlin in

59

57 BELOW LEFT Marcel Breuer: 'Wassily' chair, 1925. Breuer emulated the lightness and strength of the bicycle frame in choosing tubular steel for the construction of his cantilever chairs.
58 BELOW RIGHT K.J. Jucker and Wilhelm Wagenfeld: table lamp, 1923–4, inspired by a functional, geometric aesthetic.

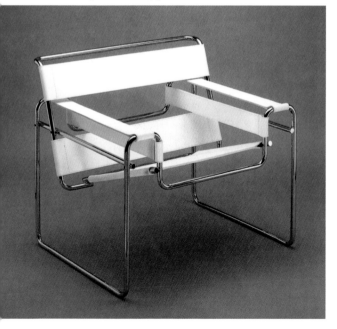

59 Grete Schütte-Lihotzky: the 'Frankfurt kitchen', 1926. Optimum working areas are provided in a room only 3.5 by 1.9 metres (11½ by 6 feet). Note the swing stool, foldaway ironing board and built-in storage that reaches the ceiling. The light could be moved along on a rail.

1922. Frederick advised on how to save time and effort in the servantless home. She ruled that the kitchen should only be used for the preparation of food, not laundry or eating, and should be as small as possible to reduce the time spent moving between appliances and work areas.

Mies's work represented the luxury end of the market, with emphasis on expensive materials. His design for the German pavilion for the Barcelona Exhibition of 1929 was unrestricted by cost or function, and he was able to experiment fully with this temporary structure. The materials were ostentatious, including brass, marble and plate glass, and were used to maximum effect, as none of the surfaces was decorated. The structure consisted of a flat slab and intersecting walls, carefully placed to allow free circulation. The monumental leather-and-chrome Barcelona chair and stool designed for the Pavilion have since become classics of modern design, and remain in production today.

60

Mies used the same spatial concept for his next domestic commission, the Tugendhat House of 1930 in Brno, Czechoslovakia. In the large living room the load is carried by slim cruciform columns covered in polished stainless steel and the interior space is divided by free-standing screens. The study is separated from the living area by a Malaga onyx partition and a semi-circular screen of Macassar ebony embraces the dining area. Mies was assisted in this as in other commissions by Lilly Reich, a German interior designer who had worked with him on the Barcelona Pavilion and ran the interior design courses at the Bauhaus during his period as director. The Tugendhat House design was typical of Mies and Reich in that it incorporated luxurious, plain materials, including silver-grey raw silk for the curtains, wool for the rug, tan and emerald-green leather and white kid for the upholstery. The flooring of white linoleum and tubular-steel furniture created an effect of stark elegance.

In 1927 Mies was involved with the first international statement of modern architecture when he directed the Deutscher Werkbund housing scheme at Stuttgart, known as the *Weissenhofsiedlung*. The city authorities provided finance for the Werkbund to design and build twenty-one model dwellings, and Mies invited fifteen leading modern architects to take part, including Gropius, Le Corbusier and the Dutch De Stijl architect J.J.P. Oud.

The exhibition put modern movement design on the map, presenting an international front for designers who shared the same aesthetic. Le Corbusier designed two dwellings for the site that expressed his 'Five Points of Architecture'. These stipulated that the building should be supported above ground level by *pilotis* (free-standing structural piers of reinforced concrete); the interior should use a free plan, unrestricted by the need for supporting walls; there should be a roof terrace; the windows should be large, and form a continuous element of the exterior wall, and the facade should consist of one smooth surface. The interior of Le Corbusier's flats consisted of a single space that could be divided to form bedrooms with the use of sliding partitions. The concept of an unrestricted internal space was basic to modern movement interior design.

German designers attempted to adapt to the needs of industry but Le Corbusier reversed the process by using machine production as an inspiration for his 'one-off' commissions. He founded the purist movement in 1918 with the painter Amedée Ozenfant (1886–1966) to celebrate a new, universal aesthetic. Le Corbusier and Ozenfant painted anonymous, mass-produced objects such as bottles and glasses in the belief that such

60 TOP Mies van der Rohe: Barcelona Pavilion and the 'Barcelona' chair and stool, 1929. The building was commissioned to be the scene of the opening ceremony performed by the Spanish King and Queen.

61 ABOVE Mies van der Rohe: dining room of the Tugendhat House, Brno, 1930. Cantilever armchairs of chromium-plated steel and silver-grey fabric, 'Tugendhat' chairs, were designed for the living area, and white kid leather-upholstered chairs, 'Brno' chairs, for the dining area.

everyday objects represented the ultimate in design, evolved over years of research and experiment. The same Darwinian process applied to architecture, and Le Corbusier sought out the simplest, most rational solution to any design problem.

Le Corbusier published his aesthetic theories in the periodical *L'Esprit Nouveau*, which he founded in 1920 with Ozenfant. He compared the elegant lines of contemporary cars with the Parthenon to demonstrate that the same aesthetic was in operation; that both represented 'type-forms', or the ultimate solution to a design problem. Whether designing furniture or replanning the whole of Paris, Le Corbusier was inspired by the same universal, absolute aesthetic. But the understanding of industrial design upon which Le Corbusier based his argument was erroneous. It has been shown that such 'type-forms' cannot exist, and that design changes in response to market forces.

Le Corbusier applied his theories to interior design at the 1925 Paris Exposition Internationale des Arts Décoratifs et Industriels Modernes. His small two-storey house, the Pavillon de l'Esprit Nouveau, challenged the nationalistic and decorative emphasis of the Exposition by including mass-produced furniture such as Thonet bentwood chairs. Many of the items were industrially produced or intended as prototypes for mass production, for instance a table made by a hospital-furniture manufacturer. All the structural components such as doors and windows were based on a modular system. The effect of the interior was deliberately sparse, with the bare walls decorated only by Léger's paintings. The main interest lay in the internal ordering, with a double-storey living area overlooked by a balcony providing a feeling of spaciousness on a very restricted site.

The Pavillon de l'Esprit Nouveau caused a great scandal at the Exposition, for it was so obviously a direct criticism of the majority of the exhibits, which celebrated the French cabinet-making tradition. Le Corbusier caused a further storm with his book *L'Art décoratif d'aujourd'hui,* published in the same year. Obviously inspired by Adolf Loos, he praised the new functional industrial design, and proclaimed that 'Modern decorative art is not decorated'. Le Corbusier argued that the best designs were the simplest. He dismissed past styles as irrelevant to the 1920s, and derided the French designers' love of luxurious materials, claiming that 'Gilt decoration and precious stones are the work of the tamed savage who is still alive in us.'

Le Corbusier's house designs of the period demonstrate the purist aesthetic. The interiors of Villa Stein at Garches (1927) and Villa Savoye at Poissy (1929–31) employ double-storey rooms, roof gardens, and ramps linking levels. They are planned as one flowing space rather than as given areas to be filled or embellished. Le Corbusier's furniture designed with Charlotte Perriand is integral, and is carefully placed to be admired aesthetically as sculpture.

The work of the partnership was seen at the Salon d'Automne in 1929 with the 'equipment of a dwelling' layout. This consisted of a single large living area with other rooms leading from it.

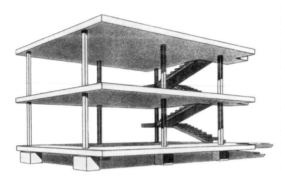

62 LEFT Le Corbusier's Maison Dom-ino, 1914, a 'building type' conceived by the architect as the basic component for industrially planned housing, demonstrating his abolition of internal supporting walls.
63 BELOW Le Corbusier: Pavillon de l'Esprit Nouveau for the Exposition des Arts Décoratifs, Paris, 1925. A double-height living room and mass-produced furniture such as Thonet bentwood chairs contrasted strongly with the rest of the French exhibits.

64 Le Corbusier: upper room and terrace, Villa Savoye, Poissy, 1929–31. The villa reveals Le Corbusier's adherence to the open-plan ideal.

The totally modern effect was achieved through the extensive use of glass and metal. The floor and ceiling was covered in glass and the furniture was made of glass, leather and tubular steel.

By 1932 the international reputation of the modern movement was established, and the Museum of Modern Art in New York held an exhibition showing plans and photographs of the work of Le Corbusier, Mies van der Rohe and Walter Gropius, together with the work of architects from Italy, Sweden, Russia, and in America. In the accompanying catalogue Henry-Russell Hitchcock and Philip Johnson aptly described the work as 'International Style', and characterized it as having flexible internal space and avoiding applied decoration. They warned against using colour on walls, adding, 'there is no better decoration for a room than a wall of book-filled shelves'. The use of plants for interior decoration was also approved.

By 1932 a handful of European immigrants had brought modern movement design to America. The system of mass production that America had pioneered and which had inspired European designers had had little effect on American interior design until the European modern movement began to make its mark there. Rudolph M. Schindler (1887–1953) and Richard Neutra (1892–1970) had arrived from Vienna to design influential

66   private houses in the European modern style. Neutra's Lovell
House in Los Angeles (1929), with its vast expanses of glass and
free internal plan was considered worthy to be included in the
Museum of Modern Art exhibition.

     Frank Lloyd Wright and other American designers could
not accept the restrictions of the modern movement, rejecting
its characteristic use of *pilotis* and regular blocks. In the 1930s
Wright continued to develop his own personal style, which he
considered more expressive of American values, culminating
67   in Fallingwater at Bear Run, Pennsylvania (1934–6). Built on a
rocky hillside, the concrete structure cantilevers over a waterfall.
The emphasis is on the organic, with rock-masonry walls, North
Carolina walnut furniture and fittings, and huge windows
creating a harmony between the natural beauty of the setting
and the interior living space. A less industrial expression of
the modern movement was also developing in Scandinavia.
Finland, Sweden and Norway had not experienced the same
rapid process of industrialization as Britain, Germany and

65 OPPOSITE Le Corbusier's and Perriand's best-known seating designs: the Chaise Longue of 1927 and (left) Grand Confort of 1928, both exhibited in 1929. Designed to express the machine aesthetic, they were never mass produced, and appealed only to a small élite.

66 RIGHT Richard Neutra: staircase, Lovell House, Los Angeles, 1929. An early example of European modernism in America. The house has a double-height living room and built-in seating. For the light on the stair-wall Neutra chose to use an off-the-shelf industrial component: a Model A Ford headlight.

67 BELOW Frank Lloyd Wright: living room, Fallingwater, Bear Run, 1934–6. The vast living area has extensive windows to integrate indoors and outdoors, and a natural stone floor.

68-9 Alvar Aalto: lecture hall, Viipuri Library, 1935. An undulating wooden ceiling and curved plywood furniture typify the more humanistic Scandinavian approach to modernism that was to be crucial for post-war interior design. Left, Aalto's chair.

America. When modern movement principles began to affect Scandinavian design around 1930 there was still a strong craft tradition in existence. Whereas in Britain arts and crafts products were too costly for most of the population to buy, Scandinavian hand-crafted goods could be bought by the majority. The simplicity of modernism was fused with folk design to produce Scandinavian modern. Furniture by Bruno Mathsson, Børge Mogensen, Kaare Klint and Magnus Stephenson was exported to America and Britain from the 1930s onwards, the softly curving lines and warmth of the woods providing a popular alternative to the coldness of German tubular steel.

The best-known exponent of Swedish modern abroad was the Finnish architect Alvar Aalto (1898–1976). Aalto's Sanatorium at Paimio (1933) and the Viipuri Library (1935), both in Finland, use brick and wood where his German contemporaries would
68　have used concrete. The undulating wooden ceiling of the lecture hall in the Viipuri Library is a superb example of Aalto's humanistic architecture. Aalto experimented with bent
69　plywood and laminates in his furniture designs of the period to achieve a modern but warm and human effect, in harmony with his interiors.

As the modern movement became accepted by the international avant-garde it acquired new political connotations. The Bauhaus had been closed down in 1932 by the Nazi-controlled Weimar council. Mies van der Rohe attempted to keep the school alive by running it as a private institution in a disused factory in the Berlin suburbs, but this too was closed by the Nazis in 1933. For the extreme Right in Germany, modern art and design represented an international, Jewish contamination of German 'Volk' culture. During the late 1930s in Germany the vernacular or the classical were the only styles deemed suitable for the expression of Third Reich ideology. Hitler's official architect Albert Speer recreated the glories of past empires in his monumental interiors, designed to intimidate and overpower.

In Italy the situation was reversed and the Fascists adopted
70　*architettura razionale* as a Party style. The Casa del Fascio at Como (1932–6) by Giuseppe Terragni (1904–1943) is a building in the International Style, with white walls and specially designed tubular-steel furniture. The link between modernism and the Right in Italy stems from the futurist movement of 1914–17, which celebrated the machine in painting, poetry, and the architectural drawings of St Elia, while welcoming the First World War as 'the hygiene of society'.

During the inter-war years the British looked on past traditions with affection, reluctant to acknowledge the nation's decline as a world power. The modern movement was slow to influence British interior design because it was regarded as foreign and left wing – an impression not entirely unfounded in view of the history of the Bauhaus – and a radical image was courted by British modernists. The powerful ideology of the 'British home' and the continuing influence of arts and crafts values almost guaranteed modernism's unpopularity. A core of convinced modernists attempted to persuade the British public and industry to accept the modernist creed, hindered no doubt by a proselytizing tone, and also by the growing popularity of a rival style that had

70 Giuseppe Terragni: Conference Room, Casa del Fascio, Como, 1932–6.

reached Britain by way of Hollywood, to be considered in the next chapter.

The British Design and Industries Association (DIA) had been founded on the model of the German Werkbund in 1915. Founder members, including the London furniture retailer Ambrose Heal of 'Heal's', the director of the Dryad furniture-manufacturing firm Harry Peach, and Heal's cousin Cecil Brewer, strove to educate the national taste. One of the DIA's propaganda exercises was the 1920 exhibition, 'Household Things', which included furniture, textiles, ceramics and glass in eight room settings. It is clear from this exhibition and from the DIA publications that the Association had a broader view than its German counterpart of what constituted 'good design'. The DIA Yearbooks, modelled on the German example, contained specimens of the Georgian Revival, and the functional aesthetic was reserved for industrial products. The DIA typified the British version of international modernism: diluted Scandinavian modern and arts and crafts traditionalism. This style can be seen in the work
71 of the furniture manufacturer and designer Gordon Russell (1892–1980), whose reconciliation of the three influences laid the foundation of 1950s British interior design.

Fleeing Nazi Germany, Walter Gropius, Marcel Breuer and the architect Erich Mendelsohn (1887–1953) all joined the avant-garde community based around Parkhill in Hampstead, London, before leaving for the United States.

British commissions for such designers were few. Gropius designed the Village College at Impington before taking up a post at Harvard. Breuer stayed from 1935 to 1937, during which time he designed bent-plywood furniture for Isokon. Mendelsohn set up in partnership with the Russian-born Serge Chermayeff (1900–1996) to design the De La Warr pavilion at Bexhill-on-Sea, Sussex (1936). Modern interior design in Britain was significantly forwarded after the appointment of designer Raymond McGrath (1908–1977) as Decoration Consultant for Broadcasting House, the new BBC headquarters. McGrath was himself an eclectic designer, and he employed Serge Chermayeff and modern architect Wells Coates (1895–1958) on his team. The interiors of the studios by Coates were outstandingly simple and functional, and used modern materials like tubular steel. The same qualities distinguished the designs for London Underground stations commissioned by Frank Pick, a founder-member of the DIA and head of the London Passenger Transport Board, from the architect Charles Holden. More than thirty tube stations were designed

71 Gordon Russell: dining room, 1933–6. Furniture in Japanese chestnut and walnut manufactured by Gordon Russell Ltd demonstrates how few concessions British design made to European modernism. The carpet is designed by Marian Pepler. (Russell Room, Geffrye Museum, London).

72 Charles Holden: London Transport Underground Station, Leicester Square, 1935. Clear design on modern principles.

on modern movement principles and were accordingly easier to use, more brightly lit, and presented a clear corporate image.

Domestic modern design was brought before the public at the 'Exhibition of British Industrial Art in Relation to the Home' in 1933. Wells Coates's 'Minimum Flat' was inspired by the topical problem of living in a small space. It contained a model kitchen, bedroom, living room and bathroom in a strictly functional modern style. The response of critics and public alike was that the Flat showed that modernism could be successful in the design of a kitchen or bathroom where efficiency was important, as well as for new types of interior such as Underground stations and broadcasting studios, but that it was not appropriate for the sanctuary of the British living room.

During the late 1930s America became the focal area for modern architecture and design. Architect-designers including Gropius, Mies van der Rohe, Marcel Breuer and Moholy-Nagy began to work and teach there, the latter to found the 'New Bauhaus' in Chicago in 1937. The modernists' achievements were to be greatly admired and emulated, particularly after the Second World War. During the 1920s and 1930s, however, there was a rival development in interior design that enjoyed far wider popularity in France, America and Britain – that of Art Deco.

72

Chapter 4
Art Deco and the Moderne

At the 1910 Bruxelles Exposition Universelle the French had exhibited interiors in the art nouveau style while the German designers showed something entirely new. Room settings by Munich-based designers such as Professor Albin Müller were simple and geometrically ordered, and showed the influence of Charles Rennie Mackintosh. Although critics referred to the austerity, restraint and peasant origins of many of the German exhibits with some disdain, it was clear that they represented a progression from the outdated art nouveau.

Later in the same year the French sense of a German challenge was confirmed at the Paris Salon d'Automne. This exhibition had been established in 1903 as a fine art showcase, but from 1906 design was included, and the 1910 exhibition featured work by Munich decorators linked with the Deutscher Werkbund, including Karl Bertsch, whose lady's bedroom was criticized by French design experts for its lack of femininity and shoddy workmanship. It nevertheless proved a popular success, and French designers were galvanized to take action to maintain the position as leaders of taste that they had enjoyed since the eighteenth century. The plan for an international exhibition concerned solely with design began to take shape.

The term 'art deco' derives from the title of this international exhibition. Because of the First World War and its aftermath the Paris Exposition Internationale des Arts Décoratifs et Industriels Modernes did not take place until 1925. The exhibition and the type of French work on display grew out of an effort to modernize French interior design in which, unusually, architecture took second place. Both art nouveau and the modern movement had been architecturally based, with interior design regarded as an inferior art. Now interior design provided the focus.

Classical inspiration, the use of smooth surfaces to envelop the three-dimensional form, love of the exotic, sumptuous materials and repeated geometric motifs characterize the art deco style. Although the style did not gain widespread recognition until 1925, its source was in the pre-war work of France's leading designers. The classicized forms of the finest French furniture of the eighteenth and nineteenth centuries had been taken as models to cleanse design of the nightmarish excesses of art nouveau.

Émile-Jacques Ruhlmann (1879–1933) was the acknowledged leader of French interior and furniture design of the period 1918 to 1925. He worked within the conventions of French eighteenth-century tradition. His architectural detailing and the proportions of his interiors were classically inspired, and his furniture designs often incorporated features associated with the Empire period such as tapered, fluted legs and drum-shaped tables. The lines of the furniture were frequently picked out with a thin ivory inlay, and delicate ivory caps, called *sabots,* covered the feet. The quality of workmanship was no less reminiscent of the eighteenth century. In common with many French art deco designers, Ruhlmann used only the rarest of materials, including lizard skin, shagreen (sharkskin, or *galuchet*), ivory, tortoiseshell and exotic hardwoods.

The market for Ruhlmann's work was necessarily restricted to the wealthy, or to such clients as the Paris Chamber of Commerce and the cosmetic firm of Yardley. To emphasize their exclusiveness, from 1928 each of his pieces was given a serial number in an edition, and a certificate with the number and Ruhlmann's signature accompanied each purchase.

73 Ruhlmann's work was displayed at the 1925 Exposition in Le Pavillon d'un Collectionneur, a series of rooms based on Ruhlmann's own house. The dining room has the classical elegance associated with Ruhlmann with chairs loosely based on the eighteenth-century *gondole* type. The vast Grand Salon of the Pavilion shows Ruhlmann working at his best. It features boldly patterned wall-coverings, a huge chandelier and classical detailing, including the entablature running around the room at the point where the walls join the ceiling.

The designers André Groult (1884–1966) and Paul Iribe (1883–1935) also used the inspiration of past French models to create a new style. Iribe was an important figure in the
76 world of French fashion who had designed an apartment for the collector of modern art and couturier Jacques Doucet in 1912 using eighteenth-century models. Groult combined the classic outlines of Louis XVI furniture with art deco features such as formalized baskets or garlands of flowers, tassels,

73 Émile-Jacques Ruhlmann: Grand Salon, Le Pavillon d'un Collectionneur, Exposition des Arts Décoratifs, Paris, 1925. The painting *Les Perruches* by Jean Dupas over the mantelpiece was a specially commissioned mural that later featured in reproduction in the sets of Cecil B. de Mille's *Dynamite* (1929).

74-5 ropes and feathers. His woman's bedroom shown in the Pavillon de l'Ambassade Française in the 1925 Exposition contained shagreen furniture such as a *bombe*-shaped chest of drawers and *gondole* chair upholstered in velvet. The sensuous curves of the chest of drawers evoke the room's intended inhabitant.

Art deco designers were not inspired solely by past French styles. A hallmark of the style is the sunrise motif, seen on the head and foot of Groult's bed. The motif was probably derived from ancient Egyptian art, a popular source of inspiration after the discovery of Tutankhamun's tomb in 1922. The geometric emphasis of much art deco was derived from cubism, the avant-garde movement in painting that lasted from *c.* 1907 to 1914. Led by Pablo Picasso and Georges Braque, it sought to deconstruct the Renaissance way of representing three dimensions on a two-dimensional surface. The new analysis of visual reality resulted in fragmented, angular forms which art deco designers assimilated into their work.

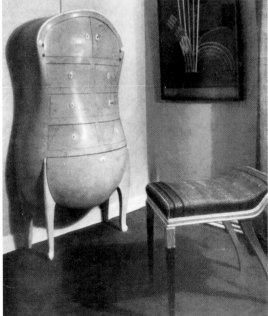

74-5 André Groult:
Chambre de Madame,
Pavillon de l'Ambassade
Française, Exposition des
Arts Décoratifs, Paris,
1925. Velvet upholstery
and a curved, shagreen-
covered chest of drawers
conjure up an ambience
of femininity. The stool
on the right of the lower
image is by Ruhlmann.

A direct link between cubism and interior design appeared in 1912 at the Salon d'Automne, when the predominantly traditional designers André Mare (1885–1932) and Louis Süe (1875–1968) collaborated with the minor cubists Roger de la Fresnaye, Raymond Duchamp-Villon and Jacques Villon on the 'Maison Cubiste'. The collaboration continued with the foundation of the decorating firm Compagnie des Arts Français in 1919 by Süe and Mare.

One of the most important inspirations for the cubists had been non-European art, and art deco designers used the same source to create the exotic ambience so characteristic of the style. The designer Pierre Legrain (1889–1929) reproduced non-Western furniture in fashionable materials. For example, the curved seat of an Ashanti stool can be identified in his exhibit at the Salon des Artistes Décorateurs of 1923, and his chair of 1924 in palmwood veneer and parchment is based on an Egyptian model.

76 Couturier Jacques Doucet's villa at Neuilly, 1929. Art deco motifs in the room illustrated include stepped ziggurat shapes on the ceiling and a desk and African tribal-inspired stool (left) by Pierre Legrain.

A taste for the exotic was also inspired by the stage designs of Léon Bakst for the Ballets Russes. Sergei Diaghilev's *Sheherazade* was seen in Paris in 1908, and the vivid colours and evocation of a distant, exotic land only heightened the contemporary fashion for Persian and Arabian themes, prompted partly by the French translation of *The Thousand and One Nights' Entertainment* between 1896 and 1904. The fashion for the oriental was also apparent in Britain and America with the craze for large tasselled cushions of varying shapes, covered in sumptuous fabrics. In June 1920 the new magazine concerned with British middle-class interiors, *Ideal Home,* described 'The Indispensable Cushions: How To Make Them and Where To Put Them'. They were used in strongly coloured rooms, often black and red, with red lacquer-work furniture and China pagoda lamps.

Avant-garde painters were experimenting with the possibilities of colour at this time, and had a marked influence on art deco. Orphism, developed in Paris before the war by Sonia and Robert Delaunay, had liberated colour from the formal concerns of easel painting. Sonia applied the experiments of orphism to design during the 1920s, decorating their apartment with square armchairs covered in geometric textiles and matching rugs, and walls hung with beige-patterned linen.

The Fauves, or 'Wild Beasts', were a group of painters including Matisse, Derain and Vlaminck whose work between 1905 and 1908 used vivid colours in shocking contrasts. Such colour combinations were adopted by designers as a reaction to the insipid pastels of art nouveau. No designer exploited the mystical East or strong colours better than Paul Poiret (1879–1944). Originally a haute-couture fashion designer renowned for liberating women from the corset, Poiret set up his own interior decoration studio, the Atelier Martine, in 1912 after seeing the work of the Wiener Werkstätte. The fauve painter Raoul Dufy (1877–1953) designed bright, fresh fabrics for the Atelier Martine from its foundation until 1912, when he left to work for the giant textile mill Bianchini-Férier. Designs were also supplied by the École Martine, a school for young working-class girls who produced the naive and colourful style of design that Poiret so admired. The Atelier successfully designed and sold printed fabrics, wallpapers, ceramics, rugs and embroideries, as well as undertaking complete interior-design commissions, including the decoration of Poiret's own couture house. The interiors relied for their effect on brightly coloured decorations of trees and flowers painted on the walls, with low furniture and shimmering or boldly patterned fabrics.

77

77 Paul Poiret: bedroom, 1924. Exotic wall decorations and a low bed with silk tasselled cushions evoke an atmosphere of the orient. To complete the fantasy a snail shell has strayed into the centre of the ceiling.

Poiret made no distinction between furnishing and clothing textiles, and this crossover between women's high fashion and interior design is typical of art deco. The style was conceived in response to the challenge of rational, functional, Austro-German design, perceived as masculine, and was identified with frivolity, irrationality and 'mere' decoration, regarded as feminine, a gender stereotype inherent in Western culture.

French women's fashion formed a dominant part of the 1925 Exposition. This was partly due to the disappointing foreign contribution. Germany did not take part, claiming that the invitation had arrived too late. America declined to contribute, as it was felt by Herbert Hoover, the Secretary of Commerce, that she could not offer examples of work that were of the 'new and really original inspiration' which the exhibition authorities had stipulated. The British showing was weak. Designed by Easton and Robertson and decorated by Henry Wilson, a vaguely Moorish structure surmounted by a model sailing ship did little to impress the French. The 1925 Exposition came only

78 Paul Follot: Grand Salon, designed for Pomone of the Paris department store Bon Marché and shown at the 1925 Exposition. The Paris stores played a major role in the development of art deco design.

a year after the Empire Exhibition at Wembley, and Britain could afford no more than a token contribution.

Most of the Exposition was made up of the French pavilions, with leading Parisian department stores making a strong showing. Many of the stores had established interior decoration departments, and their skills were displayed at the Exposition in a number of room settings in the art deco style. Paul Follot (1877–1941) became the Director of Pomone for the store Bon Marché in 1923 and Maurice Dufrêne (1876–1955) headed La Maîtrise at the Galeries Lafayette from 1921. Follot's Grand Salon for Bon Marché uses a bold contrast of angular patterns and stylized flowers on the carpet, panels of the display cabinets and entablature. Art deco interiors rarely incorporated paintings, as the decorations themselves were sufficiently rich. The one exception to this was the mural painting.

78

Murals formed an essential part of the luxurious Art Deco interior. Ruhlmann used a large work by Jean Dupas (1882–1964), *Les Perruches,* in the Grand Salon of 'Le Pavillon d'un Collectionneur'. This was typical of Dupas's work with its combination of stylized figures of women and a highly colourful background of birds, fruit and flowers. Jose-Marie Sert (1874–1945) was another such mural painter, whose commissions were on a vast scale, and who decorated ballrooms for high-society hosts. Exotic scenes were often painted in black on silver or gold leaf backgrounds, reflecting Sert's early involvement with theatrical design.

Exotic fauna and flora also figured in art deco metal furniture and fittings. Armand-Albert Rateau (1882–1938) created bizarre interiors in which strange bird shapes in bronze supported tables and even formed the bath taps. The apartment he designed for the couturier Jeanne Lanvin included a low table with patinated bronze birds supporting a marble top, set in a bedroom hung with embroidered blue silk. Edgar Brandt (1880–1960) was the leading French metalworker of the 1920s, and frequently used animals, birds and flowers in his designs. The decorative panel 'Les Cigognes d'Alsace' of 1923 features three storks in an octagon surrounded by a garland of flowers, with radiating sunbeams and spiral motifs. Copies of the panels were used to decorate lifts at the new Selfridges department store in London in 1928. Brandt contributed extensively to the 1925 Exposition, designing the wrought-iron gates in the Pavillon d'un Collectionneur.

Designers at the Exposition worked as traditional French *ensembliers,* ordering all aspects of the interior to create a

79 Armand-Albert Rateau's bedroom for the couturier Jeanne Lanvin, 1920–2. Embroidery of gold-and-white marguerites and an alcove bed create an atmosphere of refinement and luxury. Note the patinated-bronze and marble table with legs in the shape of birds. (Room reconstructed in the Musée des Arts Décoratifs, Paris).

complete work of art, symbolically expressive of the intended inhabitant. Art deco designers opposed modern movement doctrine because it neglected individuality and the decorative aspect of interior design which they felt to be so vital. Le Corbusier's display at the Exposition showed that modern movement architects believed in a universal style for all interiors, whether private or public.

This position altered after the 1925 Exposition as a new generation of French designers began to use the modern movement aesthetic in their work. The 'moderne' designers, as they came to be known, upset the old guard and Paul Follot in particular with their apparent neglect of French decorative traditions. The career of Eileen Gray (1878–1976) demonstrates this trend. In 1920 she designed an apartment for the milliner Suzanne Talbot in which animal skins, an armchair upholstered in salmon-pink with front legs modelled on two rearing serpents, a *piroque* (canoe) sofa in patinated bronze lacquer with silver-leaf decoration, and a lacquer-work brick wall leading from the gallery to the bedroom created the exotic and sumptuous atmosphere typical of art deco. In 1922 she opened her showrooms in Paris, the 'Galerie Jean Désert', to sell exclusive art deco handmade rugs and lacquer-work screens. As a result of the influence of the modern movement in the late 1920s, she became interested in architecture and abandoned her earlier highly decorative style. Her later designs were for practical tubular-steel, glass and wooden furniture. Her Transat chair of 1927, for example, is box-shaped and has chrome-steel fasteners connecting the black-lacquered frame.

Other art deco designers to follow a similar path included members of the Union des Artistes Modernes, founded in 1929 by Pierre Chareau, René Herbst, Robert Mallet-Stevens and François Jourdain among others. This group welcomed new industrial materials and modern movement ideas, in opposition to the more reactionary Société des Artistes Décorateurs. Chareau's 'Maison de Verre', 31 Rue Saint Guillaume, Paris, used standardized industrial components, including glass bricks, to create entire walls within a metal

80 OPPOSITE ABOVE Art deco modulates into the moderne. Background, left, Eileen Gray's pink chair with legs modelled on two rearing serpents, designed in 1920, the epitome of art deco. Two more functional Bibendum chairs of 1929 and a tobacco-coloured sofa, also by Gray, are moderne. Gray's former dark and sultry apartment for milliner Suzanne Talbot has been remodelled by Paul Ruaud in 1932 with a glass floor and clinical white-painted walls.
81 OPPOSITE BELOW Pierre Chareau: the 'Maison de Verre', Paris, 1932. Huge metal supports, glass bricks and non-slip rubber flooring are the setting for art deco furniture by Chareau.

frame. Although this might appear to embody the aims of the modern movement, it is, rather, the fashionable adaptation of the aesthetic. Designers like Chareau (1883–1950) incorporated modern materials and tubular-steel furniture into their designs to provide a modish effect, and cared little for the aims and ideals of Le Corbusier or the Bauhaus.

The French authorities were just as eager to exploit the prestige of French design during the 1930s as they had been during the previous decade. In 1935 the maiden voyage of the largest passenger liner in the world, the *Normandie,* provided the opportunity for France to display the best work of her designers. René Lalique (1860–1945) had experimented with the decorative possibilities of glass from the turn of the century, making scent bottles, car mascots and interior fittings. He designed glass panels, two huge chandeliers and standard lights for the 305-foot (92-metre) main dining room of the *Normandie.* Contemporary design was officially encouraged in France, and this contributed towards the success of art deco as an international decorative style. The picture was very different in Britain, where there was no such national pride in the achievements of interior designers.

82 Glass by René Lalique for a dining room designed by the Rouen painter Raymond Quibel, displayed at the Exposition des Arts Décoratifs, Paris, 1925. The furniture is exotic palissander.

83 First-class dining room of the passenger liner *Normandie*, 1935, with Lalique's vast chandeliers, thirty vertical light-panels and twelve fountains of glass supported on pedestals, a glittering showcase of French design.

Art deco and the moderne, like modernism, were slow to influence British design. After the First World War a prevailing mood of insecurity was countered by a revival of interest in the Elizabethan period, Britain's great age. This was reflected in interior design with a mania for panelled rooms and mock-Tudor electric light fittings. The pages of British publications such as *The Studio, Ideal Home* and *The Studio Yearbook of Decorative Art* for this period are filled with images of traditional English cottages with cosy interiors, supplied with mock-Jacobean furniture and chintz upholstery – revivals that owed as much to the national mood as to the lingering influence of the arts and crafts movement.

In 1911 Marcel Boulestin had opened a decorating shop called 'Decoration Moderne' in Elizabeth Street, London, supplying textiles and wallpaper by Studio Martine, André Groult and Iribe, but this had little effect on majority taste. *The Studio* magazine criticized much of the 1925 Exposition as pursuing novelty for its own sake. French progressive furniture was first seen in London in 1928 when the decorating firm of Shoolbred's held an exhibition of work by DIM (Décoration Intérieure Moderne), a company that had been founded in

84 Serge Chermayeff: dining room of his own house, London, 1930. A moderne combination of tubular steel and highly polished veneer, rare in 1930s Britain.

1919 by René Joubert. In the same year the furniture company Waring & Gillow opened a Modern Art Department in London for the sale of French and British furniture under the direction of Paul Follot and Chermayeff. Chermayeff's sixty-eight room settings for the exhibition reflected Parisian taste for veneered and highly polished furniture, patterned floor coverings and geometric motifs. Chermayeff created a similar effect in the living room and dining room of his own home, which included such 'moderne' features as tubular-steel chairs. In this and his architectural commissions he was able to combine his knowledge of the modern with French developments to produce a successful blend. From 1928 onwards, British design generally became less insular as contemporary trends from the Continent were seen and discussed.

84

The chief source of the moderne inspiration, however, was America. Isolated from Europe during the 1914–18 war, Americans first learned of advances in design from the 1925 Paris Exposition. Up to this point only styles evoking past periods had been used. There was the American arts and crafts movement which had survived the First World War, with the Mission Revival (1890–1915) and the Spanish Colonial Revival (1915–1930) forming a part of this trend. America regarded her achievements in the decorative arts with such small esteem that, while she did not participate in the 1925 Paris Exposition, a large contingent of more than one hundred American delegates attended, representing every design field. Most were favourably impressed by what they saw. The new French style was disseminated in America by magazines and museum and store displays. In 1926 the Metropolitan Museum of Art, New York, organized a touring exhibition of design artefacts, and established a permanent gallery for the display of furniture bought at the Paris Exposition. New York department stores, most notably Saks, Fifth Avenue, Macy's and Lord and Taylor, set up displays of contemporary French furniture after 1925. No fewer than thirty-six museums and department stores held exhibitions of art deco throughout America during the next three years.

Art deco was enthusiastically received because it was new, not retrospective, and America, as a comparatively young country, was anxious to establish a distinctive design identity to match her economic and industrial presence. America had led the world in methods of mass production and marketing manufactured goods. Art deco style's bright surfaces and abstract patterns well expressed American aspirations, not least in the suggestion of machine production contained in the precise repetition of geometric motifs. Ironically, the ease with which art deco was assimilated could also be explained by the continuing authority of Paris as a leader of taste.

85   The Viennese-born designer Joseph Urban (1872–1933) had established the Wiener Werkstätte of America, opening a showroom on Fifth Avenue, New York, to produce finely crafted, geometrically based furniture in the spirit of the Austrian prototype. The Werkstätte only lasted from 1922 to 1924, but Urban's designs for simple chairs with repetitive square decoration made the Americans more receptive to art deco. Urban used art deco for the design of pavilions at the 1933 'Century of Progress' exhibition in Chicago, including the Travel and Transport Building, which used the rising sun motif combined with the stepped ziggurat shape of the style. Art deco was soon adopted for the interiors of buildings as

diverse as modest hotels in Miami Beach and skyscrapers in
New York City. The skyscraper had emerged as a building type
in New York during the 1870s, and had flourished in Chicago
during the next decade. During the inter-war years skyscrapers
were built at a great rate in every major American city. The
designs for the foyers of these buildings needed to measure
up to their imposing exteriors.

Ely Jacques Kahn (1884–1972) was the leading designer of
art deco skyscraper entrance lobbies, including the Lefcourt
Clothing Center, 120 Wall Street, and the Bricken Building,
111 John Street, of the late 1920s. The interiors of the Chrysler
Building (1928–30) and the Empire State Building (1930–32)
are resplendent with art deco motifs: the entire surface of
the elevator doors of the Chrysler Building is veneered in light
amber and dark brown woods in a geometric lotus design.
The lighting fixtures, signs and floors are all decorated with
stylized flowers and geometrical shapes taken straight from
86 the 1925 Exposition. Another important skyscraper, the Chanin
Building, on 42nd Street and Lexington Avenue, New York,
was built during 1928–9 as a monument to the success of
property developer Irwin S. Chanin. The interior decoration
was overseen by Jacques Delamarre, head of the huge Chanin
87 Construction Company. The opulent Executive Suite washroom,
created for Irwin S. Chanin, was tiled in cream, gold and green

85 OPPOSITE Joseph Urban:
'Man's Den' for the 'Architect
and the Industrial Arts' exhibition,
New York's Metropolitan Museum,
1929. Severe geometrical design
sparked by the patterned rug.
86 ABOVE LEFT Lobby of the
Chanin Building, New York.
Plaque 'Endurance' and art
deco metal grille by René
Paul Chambellan and Jacques
Delamarre, 1928–9. The plaque
is one of a series 'New York –
City of Opportunity'.
87 ABOVE RIGHT Washroom for
Irwin S. Chanin, 52nd storey,
Chanin Building, New York,
1928–9. Note the art deco
sunburst over the engraved-
glass shower doors.
88 RIGHT Light fitting of
cast aluminium inspired by
contemporary skyscraper
design, Weary & Alford,
City Hall, Kalamazoo, c. 1930.

Art Deco and the Moderne

with a gold-plated sunburst over the geometrically engraved glass shower doors.

French art deco also strongly influenced the interiors of the Netherland Plaza Hotel, Carew Tower, Cincinnati, of 1931 by Walter W. Ahlschlager (recently restored). The lavish Hall of Mirrors and Palm Court have ornamental metalwork balustrades in the style of Edgar Brandt, with exquisite glass and metal lamps. The luxurious foyer of the Banking Hall of the Irving Trust Company, New York (1932), was one of the last grand interiors to be designed in a purely art deco manner in America. The vast walls are decorated with a reflective mosaic in red shading to orange. The vertical line is emphasized by

89 Foyer of the Banking Hall of the Irving Trust Company, New York City, by Ralph Walker of Voorhees, Gmelin & Walker, 1932.

90 Walter Dorwin Teague: sitting room for La Société Matford, Paris, late 1930s. The verticals of the skyscraper lobby give way to streamlining.

the panels that divide the walls, and by the perpendicular heating vents.

The vertical so characteristic of art deco was to give way to the horizontal line during the 1930s, as another design trend emerged in America that was to combine elements of art deco, the International Style and French moderne. This was streamlining, or the American moderne.

As a result of the 1929 Wall Street Crash American manufacturers found themselves compelled to stimulate new markets for their products. Design grew in importance as it was recognized as a marketing tool. Individual designers began to enjoy almost film-star status as manufacturers discovered that design sold goods. Norman Bel Geddes (1893–1958), Henry Dreyfuss (1904–1972) and Walter Dorwin Teague (1883–1960) were just three of the new breed of designers who established practices devoted to the design of everything from cameras and fridges to ocean liners and trains. Their concern for the total look of any design can be traced back to the example of the French *ensemblier*. Streamlining was the style in which such designers chose to work.

90

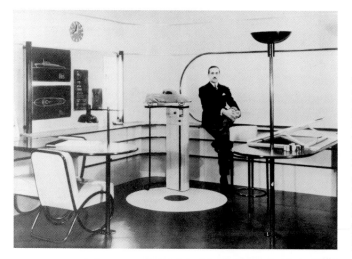

91 LEFT An industrial designer's office, with its designer. Raymond Loewy in his mock-up for the 'Contemporary American Industrial Art' exhibition, Metropolitan Museum of Art, New York, 1934.

92 BELOW 'Great Workroom' of the Johnson Wax Building, Racine, Wisconsin, designed and furnished by Frank Lloyd Wright in 1936–9.

Adopting shapes developed in experiments with aerodynamics in cars and trains, the American moderne grew out of a need to express the new dynamism of American life. It combined the sleek surfaces of art deco, the French moderne preference for new materials, and an optimistic view of machinery inspired by the Italian futurist movement and America's own Stuart Davis, who rendered the excitement of American mass culture in paint. In an America recovered from the severe blow of the Wall Street Crash, a new optimism and faith in the future prevailed. Less restricted by tradition than Europe, American society freely adopted streamlining for every domestic and public purpose. Because of its aerodynamic source and emphasis on the horizontal, interiors in the style often had three horizontal bands running round the walls. Also rooted in aerodynamics were the teardrop shape and smooth rounded corners.

Early examples can be seen in the new designs for trains. Beginning with the Union Pacific Railroad's 'City of Salina' of 1934 (produced by the Pullman Car and Manufacturing Company) and culminating in Dreyfuss's '20th Century Limited' of 1938 for New York Central, the trains were styled with bullet-shaped fronts and horizontal banding to symbolize the airflow as the train sped along. For the interior, Dreyfuss used venetian blinds and horizontal bands at the top of columns and on the metal lampshades to carry the airstream motif through. New materials and finishes were also important to the style. In '20th Century Limited' Dreyfuss gave a moderne look with coloured metallic finishes, cork panelling and plastic laminates.

Streamlining began as an appropriate style for transport, but was applied to all areas of design during the 1930s, from kitchen appliances like irons to office equipment. Raymond Loewy's 'Model Office and Studio for an Industrial Designer', designed for the Metropolitan Museum's 1934 exhibition 'Contemporary American Industrial Art', is made almost entirely from ivory-coloured plastic laminate and blue gunmetal. Again, the horizontal is emphasized with three metal bands running round the room. All the lines are curved, including the window frames and furniture, to give the whole interior an effect of smoothness.

Frank Lloyd Wright used the same moderne style for his Johnson Wax Building, Racine, Wisconsin (1936–9). The vast main office space is punctuated by support columns that are stepped outwards in ziggurat-shape as they approach the ceiling and meet a circular pad which separates the areas of overhead lighting. The metal furniture Wright designed for

91

92

the office echoes the motif with circles and horizontal bands. The interior of New York City's Radio City Music Hall (1933), largely by designer Donald Deskey (1894–1989), is a particularly fine example of the application of streamlining to a commercial interior. Clean smooth lines, mirrors, chromium-plated steel and tubular aluminium furniture, veneers, Bakelite and lacquer are used to create an atmosphere of glamour and luxury.

The sleek surfaces of the moderne and streamlining were fully exploited by the American motion picture industry, for the moderne style matched the buoyantly confident mood of inter-war Hollywood. In the early days of cinema, sets were merely theatrical backdrops adapted for black-and-white presentation. By 1915 the profession of 'art director' had been created, reflecting the influence of European experimental art, architecture and theatre, particularly expressionism. Cedric Gibbons, one of the first art directors, described his role with modesty in 1938: 'The audience should be aware of only one thing – that the settings harmonize with the atmosphere of the story and the type of character in it.' Inspired by a visit to the 1925 Paris Exposition, in *Grand Hotel* (MGM, 1932) Gibbons created sumptuous interiors with satin bed covers and wall-hangings, moderne furniture and mirrors as the appropriate setting for the star of the film, Greta Garbo. But it was for the musical that the most lavish sets were created, Busby Berkeley's *Gold Diggers of 1933* (MGM, 1933) and films starring Fred Astaire and Ginger Rogers – for example *Top Hat* (RKO, 1935) – made full use of reflective surfaces, long sweeping curves and ziggurat outlines. The impact of such *mise en scènes* on interior design at all levels was immense.

Cinema attendance in Britain reached a peak between the wars. Most adults visited the cinema at least once a week during the days of the Depression, when an evening of Hollywood films offered warmth and escapist glamour. The Hollywood cinema and the moderne style as a whole inspired a generation of British architect-designers to dispense with period detailing like picture rails, cornices and dados. Smooth, clean surfaces were emphasized with mirrors or reflective materials such as silver foil, paint or metal. When in 1930 the Australian architect-designer Raymond McGrath (1903–1977) refurbished a Victorian

93 OPPOSITE ABOVE Donald Deskey: private apartment for the manager of Radio City Music Hall, New York City, 1933. An outstanding example of the American moderne, with exotic cherrywood panelling and furniture of lacquered and veneered wood, Bakelite and brushed aluminium.
94 OPPOSITE BELOW Donald Deskey: dining room for Abbey Rockefeller Milton, Manhattan, 1933–4. 'Silver glazed' walls, Macassar ebony table and white leather for the chairs recall the French designers' love of rich materials.

95 Hollywood movies spread the message of the American moderne: 'Our Dancing Daughters', 1928. Set designed by art director Cedric Gibbons, with French art deco pillowed divan and Hollywood-style stepped screen.

house in Cambridge, he renamed it 'Finella' after the Scottish queen who built a glass palace. The interior was entirely reflective. The entrance-hall floor was covered with black induroleum, the walls were silver-leaf sprayed with green lacquer, and the ceiling covered with green glass. The pilasters were green cast sheet-glass banded in chromium and lit from within. The architect Basil Ionides (1884–1950) designed the Savoy Theatre, London, in 1929 with an auditorium decorated in silver-leaf picked out in different shades of gold lacquer.

The architect-designer Oliver Hill (1887–1968), admired for his more historicist work in the 1920s, became a convinced moderne designer in the 1930s. He carried the reflective surface to its furthest extreme in designing an all-glass display for Pilkington Brothers (the major glass manufacturers) at the furniture exhibition at Dorland Hall, London, in 1933. The floor was made up of glass tiles with gold and mirrored mosaic, the walls were decorated glass panels, and the furniture was made of plate glass. Hill's design of *c.* 1931 for the entrance hall of Gayfere House, London, for Lady Mount

Temple, consisted of mirror-glass from ceiling to floor with a gleaming wooden floor and illuminated pillars.

Lighting became important in itself during the development of the inter-war interior. Chermayeff's design for the Cambridge Theatre, London, and Oliver Percy Bernard's (1881–1939) foyer of the Strand Palace Hotel, London, both of 1930, use lighting as an architectural element. In the Cambridge Theatre coloured, geometrically patterned glass screens are used to conceal the light source. In the Strand Palace Hotel, columns and stairs seem composed entirely of strips of light. Such devices were used particularly for the design of new building types, most notably cinemas.

Some cinema interiors were based loosely on classical models, but the majority were moderne. Trent and Lewis's New Victoria Cinema in London of 1929 is typical, with fan-shaped columns dramatized by concealed lighting. The Odeon chain, designed mainly by H.W. Weedon (1887–1970) between 1934 and 1939, used art deco motifs to great effect, particularly shiny surfaces

96 Oliver Percy Bernard: foyer entrance, Strand Palace Hotel, London, 1930. Lighting used as an architectural element.

and Egyptian or Assyrian patterns, ziggurat outlines, bright-coloured squares or scrolls and geometric figures.

The cheapness of electricity had encouraged its use in interior design and also opened up a mass market for domestic consumer goods. A number of new factories were constructed on Western Avenue, one of the main routes out of London, for American clients by Thomas Wallis, Gilbert & Partners. The Hoover Factory (1932) is a symmetrical, classical-style building with bold moderne decoration. The main entrance is dominated by a coloured glass sunburst, symbol of energy and modernity, and the boardroom inside the building looks out through the top half of this imposing window. The style of the factory was an important ingredient of the corporate image, and in Britain as elsewhere, the use of the moderne denoted a progressive and successful company. The pure International Style's message of ultra-modernity and democratic functionalism was understood by few at this period.

98   In Britain art deco and the moderne gained mass appeal in the later 1930s. The four million homes built between 1919 and 1939 in England and Wales were typically modest-sized, semi-detached, and located in the suburbs. Tudor Revival is the most commonly used style, with half-timbering outside, and such motifs as galleons in stained glass in the panes of the windows. Combined with these are lively art deco motifs, particularly the rising sun, which figured on garden gates, in the window-glass and particularly on radio cabinets. The three-piece suite was a new feature of the middle-class lounge; it consisted of a two- or three-seater couch and two armchairs, thickly upholstered to suggest comfort, and covered with leather, velveteen or moquette, which might be decorated with moderne geometric designs. The glazed china cabinet was often used to display the best tea service. The 'Crocus' design tea-set by Clarice Cliff (1899–1972), for example, consisted of angular-shaped pieces, cream coloured and decorated with vivid triangular patterns in bright orange and black.

Art deco and the moderne had an equally pervasive influence on the American domestic interior during the inter-war years, until by the end of the 1930s America enjoyed a confidence in the creation of a style that owed little to European models. Paul T. Frankl, a Viennese-born designer who had emigrated to America, proclaimed in *New Dimensions* (1928) that 'new ground has been broken and the foundation for a distinctive American

98 ABOVE Popular
art deco: a suburban
lounge. Wooden
fittings from a house
of c. 1937 with the
authentic furniture
(Geffrye Museum,
London).
99 LEFT Paul T.
Frankl: sitting room,
displayed at Abram
& Strauss, New York,
1929. A 'Skyscraper'
bookcase mirrors
the burgeoning
Manhattan skyline.

art is already being laid'. He celebrated this belief in his own
99   designs for 'Skyscraper Furniture', inspired by the building-
type that American architects had invented and developed
independently of Europe. In a more conservative vein,
Americans were also responsible for founding and nurturing
the profession devoted to the overall look of a room, that of
interior decorator.

Chapter 5
The Emergence of Interior Decoration as a Profession

Before the twentieth century the profession of 'interior decoration' simply did not exist. Traditionally it was the upholsterer, cabinetmaker or retailer who advised on the arrangement of interiors. In London, the firm of Lenygon and Morant, founded in 1915, was typical. Francis Lenygon was primarily a furniture dealer, supplying chiefly Americans through the art dealer Joseph Duveen. His decorating work was a marginal part of the business he shared with Morant, the traditional upholsterer. Their London showroom was situated in a Palladian house, and was used to display English antique furniture from the sixteenth to mid-eighteenth centuries, when, it was generally considered, the production of 'good' furniture came to an end. Twentieth-century interior decorators consistently worked within the styles of the past, and until the First World War decorating was almost synonymous with the antique trade.

The rise of the interior decorator during the twentieth century was the result of changed social and economic circumstances. The employment of an interior decorator was, and remains, an expensive luxury, available only to the upper echelons of society. There is a certain status attached to using a professional to advise on the appearance of your home or workplace. During the early years of the century American millionaires sought to express power and prestige by using professional decorators to recreate Renaissance palaces or French châteaux. In the 1920s and 1930s, the heyday of the decorator, there was a greater emphasis than ever before on entertaining, and decorators were employed to create suitable backdrops for the lavish cocktail parties then fashionable. Their services remained in demand during the Depression because it was cheaper to redecorate an existing house than build a new one.

The role of interior decorator has always been one of adviser and even confidante. Because of the consultative nature of the work it has been one of the few professions in which women have led and excelled. In the years preceding the First World War interior decoration emerged as an acceptable new profession for women.

Inspired by the suffragette movement in America, women strove to establish economic independence from husbands or fathers, and one of the means open to them was the orchestration of the overall appearance of pre-existing rooms. This role has changed little since the 1900s. Decorators are chiefly responsible for selecting suitable textiles, floor- and wall-coverings, furniture, lighting and an overall colour scheme for rooms that may already contain some of these elements. The interior decorator is rarely responsible for structural alterations, which are the preserve of the architect.

Interior decoration never enjoyed the status of architecture or even interior design, being regarded as a branch of fashion. This could be explained by its ephemeral nature, for few schemes remain intact for any length of time. The lack of seriousness associated with interior decoration could also be explained by the dominance of women in the profession's early days. The Victorian middle-class woman was expected to stay at home and manage the household and servants. The decoration of the domestic interior was a respectable pastime that allowed women some control over their environment. Periodicals such as *Home Chat* (1895–1968), as well as various home manuals, advised on the selection of furniture and furnishings and the application of decorating techniques such as stencilling. As Jacob von Falke, vice-director of the Austrian Museum of Art and Industry, described the position in the popular American edition of *Art in the House* (1879): 'taste in woman may be said to be natural to her sex. She is the mistress of the house in which she orders like a queen.'

The extension of the traditional female role into professional practice began in America, where women were less restricted by established codes of behaviour. Candace Wheeler (1827–1923) was an American textile designer who did much to further the cause of women's professional employment when in 1877 she established the New York Society of Decorative Art to educate women and find outlets for their handicrafts. As Wheeler commented, the new Society 'opened the door to honest effort among women', and, 'if it was narrow, it was still a door ... the idea of *earning* had entered into the minds of women'. In 1879

Wheeler went on to establish L.C. Tiffany and Associated Artists with Louis Comfort Tiffany, the son of the founder of Tiffany and Co., and in 1883 she formed a breakaway company run entirely by women, Associated Artists, which became one of the most successful decorating firms in America, designing interiors, wallpaper, fabrics and embroidery in a style inspired by the British arts and crafts and aesthetic movements. She shared the secret of her success in the book *Principles of Home Decoration With Practical Examples* (1903), and publicized her encouragement of professionals in an article entitled 'Interior Decoration as a Profession for Women' in *The Outlook* magazine in 1895. This marked the beginning of the social acceptability of such a career for women.

Interior decoration gained status with the publication in 1897 of *The Decoration of Houses* by the future novelist Edith Wharton and architect Ogden Codman. The book set a precedent for all subsequent decorating activity by equating 'natural good taste' with English, Italian and French models from the Renaissance onwards. There was particular emphasis in the book on French eighteenth-century interiors which was to inspire a lasting admiration among decorators and their

100 The 'Old French look'. Ogden Codman Jr: parlour for the future novelist Edith Wharton, New York, c. 1903.

clients for the 'Old French look'. The comparative simplicity of Louis XV, Louis XVI and Directoire furniture was preferred to the overblown revivalism of the later nineteenth century. The

100

parlour designed by Ogden Codman for Wharton at 884 Park Avenue, New York City, had a marked freshness and simplicity, achieved with austere striped wallpaper and upholstery and painted Directoire furniture. Wharton and Codman identified the principles of proportion and harmony as the most significant for the planning of interior schemes. Taken from classical architecture, such laws have had an enduring appeal for the decorator. During the late nineteenth century classicism had been identified as the most appropriate style to symbolize the American Republic. It evoked qualities of solidity, endurance and universal harmony.

The craft of the interior decorator became associated with the elegant, if not entirely accurate, recreation of antique interiors. Such historicism was inextricably bound up with the notion of 'good taste', which the decorator possessed by virtue of studying the decorative styles of the past and being a member of the same social circles as his or her patrons. The criterion of 'good taste' was to dominate the profession throughout the twentieth century, with decorators rarely designing wholly modern interiors. *The House Beautiful* magazine included a long-running series entitled 'The House in Good Taste', and numerous books appeared on the subject, including *Furnishing the Home in Good Taste* (1912) by Lucy Abbot Throop, *Good Taste in Home Decoration* (1954) by Donald D. MacMillen, and in 1968 a contribution by Britain's leading decorator, David Hicks: *On Living – With Taste.*

Elsie de Wolfe (1865–1950), a pioneer of the profession of interior decoration in America, contributed to the trend in 1913 with her book *The House in Good Taste,* which included the advice that 'It is the personality of the mistress that the home expresses. Men are forever guests in our homes, no matter how much happiness they may find there.' De Wolfe began her professional life as an actress, attracting attention less by her performances than her dress sense, bringing the latest Parisian creations of Paquin and the House of Worth to New York. By her own efforts she gained an entrée to New York high society, at that time dominated by the Vanderbilts.

Her earliest foray in 1897–8 was the decoration of the house she shared with wealthy theatrical agent Elisabeth Marbury

101-2

in Irving Place, New York City. She was inspired to bring 'light, air and comfort' to the dark, cramped Victorian interior by the writing of Wharton and Codman. During the last two decades of the nineteenth century there had been a general

101-2 Elsie de Wolfe's dining room at Irving Place, New York City, before redecoration in 1896, and transformed in 1898.

move among the upper classes towards a greater restraint in interior decoration, as the trappings of the resplendent mid-nineteenth-century parlour became available to their social inferiors through mass production and a higher standard of living. The American breakfast-cereal magnate Dr John Harvey Kellogg had contributed to the trend when he inspired a whole health-reform movement with his writings, which castigated fashionable excesses as unhealthy.

De Wolfe revitalized the interior by stripping away the Victorian features. She removed the gasolier, decorative plates, oil painting, rococo mirror, and the jumble of oriental carpets. After redecoration the room was lit by sconces mounted against simple white-framed mirrors. She placed a plainer mirror and classical French bust over the mantelpiece. The floor was covered with a single unpatterned carpet. The room was made considerably lighter by painting the woodwork pale grey, and substituting more elegant painted chairs of Louis XVI type. The rest of the house was treated in the same way. A constant stream of high society, literary and artistic visitors

103 Elsie de Wolfe: Trellis Room, Colony Club, New York City, begun 1905. From *The House in Good Taste,* 1913. French inspiration for the trellised 'country look'

was impressed by her transformation of what had been a mediocre interior.

The leading New York Beaux-Arts architect, Stanford White, admired De Wolfe's achievements, and in 1905 secured for her the contract for the interior decoration of his building for New York City's Colony Club, a new club open only to women members. This was the first public interior to be designed by a professional interior decorator, rather than by an architect or antique dealer. De Wolfe was inspired by the elegant rooms she had seen in English country houses in the 1880s. She visited both England and France to acquire suitable antique furniture and samples of the chintzes that were to become her trademark. The bedrooms, private dining room and library all had the same refined look. The walls were painted in pale tones, the furniture was mainly slender and light, and the large prints of the chintzes added an English country atmosphere. In the tea room the green-painted trellis work, tiled floor and wicker furniture evoked a conservatory rather than a city-centre club.

De Wolfe's scheme was a success and guaranteed her further commissions. The most prestigious of these came from the millionaire Henry Clay Frick. On a visit to Hertford House, the former London residence of Sir Richard Wallace (now the Wallace Collection), Frick had been impressed by the display of eighteenth-century French fine and decorative art, recently bequeathed to the nation. Determined to found a similar institution in America, Frick commissioned the architects Carrère and Hastings to design a Renaissance palace on Fifth Avenue, New York City, to house an extensive collection of eighteenth-century French art which he formed with the advice of the English picture- and antique-dealer Edward Duveen. Duveen's English decorator William Allom was responsible for the public area on the ground floor. Frick commissioned De Wolfe to decorate the upper floor, used only by his close family. She worked for a ten per cent commission of costs, and it appears that these totalled over one million dollars. Most of De Wolfe's purchases were made in Paris from Lady Victoria Sackville-West, who had inherited a premier collection of French antiques, assembled by Wallace, from her lifelong friend, the connoisseur Sir John Murray Scott. The Frick commission made De Wolfe's name, and she went on to decorate numerous interiors for America's wealthy families.

Elsie de Wolfe established the working pattern for subsequent interior decorators. Her trips to Europe to gather antique furniture and fabrics, the extensive social contacts with potential clients, her adherence to the Wharton and Codman approach and taste for the 'Old French', set a standard. A group of professional decorators emerged during the 1920s and 1930s in America and England, eager to emulate her success. Nancy McClelland (1876–1959) established the decorating section for Wanamakers department store, New York, in 1913, the first of its type in America, and in 1922 went on to establish a decorating firm that specialized in the accurate recreation of period interiors for the domestic market and museums. Eleanor McMillen (1890–1991, known as Eleanor McMillen Brown from 1935) worked within the same classical idiom, and founded McMillen Inc. in 1924 as 'the first professional full-service interior decorating firm in America'. She had taken courses in art history and business practice, and was determined not to be identified with the rather amateurish approach of her contemporaries. The firm survives into the twenty-first century, with characteristic interiors using acid yellow to offset symmetrically placed antique furniture. In a commission for

104-5

Mrs Millicent Rogers in New York, McMillen brought the classic decorator's features of black-and-white checked floor, *trompe l'oeil* details on the walls and symmetrically placed antique furniture to the hall, where a European, late nineteenth-century sofa upholstered in satin looks ill at ease. Wealthy Americans lacked confidence in their own cultural heritage, and generally looked to European models.

Ruby Ross Wood (1881–1950) was an admirer of De Wolfe who began her professional life as a journalist, ghost-writing De Wolfe's *Ladies' Home Journal* articles which became *The House in Good Taste.* Wood established herself as an interior decorator with the publication of her own book, *The Honest House* (1914), which illustrated the interiors of her Forest Hills Gardens home at Long Island. She was inspired by eighteenth-century English and American Colonial models, rather than the sophisticated French antiques favoured by De Wolfe and others. This trend had been encouraged by the 1876 Philadelphia Centennial Exhibition and the Chicago Columbian Exhibition of 1893, and gained further momentum from the opening of the American Wing at the Metropolitan Museum of Art, New York, in October 1924 with its sixteen period rooms.

After running Au Quatrième for Wanamakers, Wood established her own decorating firm in the 1920s. Her design for Swan House, Atlanta, Georgia (1928), for Mrs Emily Inman combined the restraint of fine antiques with the homeliness of the Colonial style. In the dining room she juxtaposed a bold check curtain with an eighteenth-century hand-painted wallpaper. The room was furnished with a rococo mirror, console tables and antique tea-caddies to recreate an eighteenth-century Colonial interior. Frances Ad;er Elkins (1888–1953),

104-5 Eleanor McMillen (Brown): hall and sitting room for Mrs Millicent Rogers, New York, late 1920s. The wall treatment of hanging textiles (right) was inspired by the French Empire style, which in turn was taken from Roman sources.

the sister of Beaux-Arts architect David Adler, was another decorator who mixed American traditional styles with French and English antiques. Her own adobe house, Casa Amesti, in Monterey, California (1918), successfully combined European antiques with traditional Spanish Colonial features such as rough plasterwork, bare floorboards and exposed ceilings. The house attracted widespread admiration, and she designed domestic interiors throughout Chicago and California in the same mode.

106

Women also played an important role in founding the profession of interior decoration in Britain. Betty Joel (1896–1985) established her own furniture-making and interior decoration business after the First World War, eventually opening a showroom in Knightsbridge with twelve room settings. She was inspired by art deco to create bold designs such as ziggurat-shaped bookcases and curved sofas. Her interiors reflected the geometrical inspiration of art deco mingled with the smoothness and glamour of the moderne, as in the all-silver bedroom at Elveden Hall, Suffolk. The firm undertook a wide variety of commercial decorating work for

106 Betty Joel: characteristically unconventional moderne chaise longue, and her patterned rug. From Derek Patmore, *Colour Schemes for the Modern Home*, London, 1933.

shops, hotels and boardrooms. In contrast, the two women who contributed most towards the establishment of interior decoration in Britain, Syrie Maugham (1879–1955) and Lady Sybil Colefax (1875–1950), worked largely on private commissions.

Syrie Maugham was the wife first of Henry Wellcome, the founder of the pharmaceutical firm, and then of the novelist Somerset Maugham. After the end of her second marriage she learned the basics of the trade by working under Ernest Thornton Smith, head of Fortnum and Mason's antique department, and went on to become the most fashionable interior decorator in London.

Like Elsie de Wolfe, with whom she had visited India, Maugham created elegant interiors using eighteenth-century French furniture with elements of the moderne and light colours. She created the fashion for 'pickling' furniture – that is, stripping antique chairs and tables of their original dark polish and finishing them with light paint or wax. Her distinctive style is best exemplified by the influential 'All-

107

107 Syrie Maugham: 'All-White' drawing room for her own house, London, c. 1929–30. The society decorator's most famous project. The low sofa covered in beige silk, low table, screens, and especially 'white on white' decor were to be strongly influential.

White' interior she created for her London house in *c.* 1929–30. The dining room had stripped-pine panelling and a floor-length ivory tablecloth. Tones of white and cream were used for the drawing-room upholstery, curtains, and an abstract rug commissioned from Marion Dorn. Three Louis XV chairs were painted off-white, and a moderne touch was added with a chromium-and-mirror screen. Maugham produced all-white

108 LEFT Syrie Maugham: interior at Wilsford Manor, near Amesbury, Wiltshire, mid-1930s. Design for the country house of the artist, poet and aesthete the Hon. Stephen Tennant.

109 BELOW Rex Whistler: 'Painted Room', Port Lympne, Kent, 1930–2. Brilliant *trompe l'œil* paintwork simulates striped fabric, with the witty addition of genuine tassels. The furniture was chiefly designed by the architect of the house, Philip Tilden.

rooms for her clients, including a bedroom for Mrs Tobin Clark at a house designed by David Adler in San Mateo, California (1930). Her commissions included interiors for Noël Coward, Mrs Wallis Simpson and the Prince of Wales.

Maugham created idiosyncratic interiors, mixing the Parisian moderne with the antique. Her rival Lady Sybil Colefax created very English interiors, inspired by the chintz and solid furniture of the English country house. She had turned from life as a London hostess to become a professional decorator in 1933, after losing money in the Wall Street Crash. In 1938 she took on a partner, John Fowler (1906–1977), an expert on eighteenth-century decoration and one of the most influential figures for the period decoration of houses.

The historical inspiration for decor was prevalent in Britain in the 1930s. An increased awareness of the value of the British heritage had been inspired in part by scholarly activity in the area of historic buildings, and public interest was heightened by magazines such as *Country Life* (founded 1897), and by the National Trust. Many of the clients who commissioned work from interior decorators themselves lived in historic buildings, and wished to maintain or recreate the authentic interiors. Fowler fulfilled their requirements with his expert advice on curtaining, paint colours, finishes, floor coverings and furniture. During the post-war years Fowler was responsible for the restoration of a number of significant British interiors, including 44 Berkeley Square, designed by William Kent, the Adam interiors of Syon House, Middlesex, and James Wyatt's Cloisters at Wilton House, Wiltshire. Such schemes and his work on properties for the National Trust needed to be historically accurate, but the smaller-scale interiors he decorated bear his individual stamp. The sitting room for the Countess of Haddington at Tyninghame in Lothian, Scotland, is characteristic with rich curtaining, chintz, heavy fringing, pyramid-shaped bookcases and chandelier. Rooms such as this were featured in British and foreign periodicals throughout Fowler's career, and contributed markedly to the popularity of the English country house look from the 1930s onwards. The British mural-painter Rex Whistler (1905–1944) worked in a number of English country houses during the inter-war years, as well as the Tate Gallery Restaurant in London, where he painted *The Expedition in Pursuit of Rare Meats* (1924–5), and his recreations of eighteenth-century scenes charmed English society. In the dining room at Plas Newydd for Lord Anglesey (1936–8) he used *trompe l'oeil* techniques on the ceiling and end walls, and painted a romanticized classical harbour scene on the long wall facing the windows.

109

110 Emilio Terry with Charles de Beistigui: roof terrace of the Beistigui apartment, Paris, 1930.

While some British decorators were excelling in recreating the past, others in Britain, France and America were finding novel sources of inspiration, such as surrealism, for the creation of witty rooms. The surrealist movement began in 1924 with the publication of the Manifesto du Surréalisme in Paris. Surrealist painters including René Magritte and Salvador Dalí attempted to illustrate the threatening world of the subconscious in their paintings, most often by juxtaposing incongruous elements within the picture frame to startle the viewer and undermine everyday expectations. The surrealist influence first came to the fore in Paris, where surrealism had been conceived. The Mexican millionaire collector Charles de Beistigui had commissioned an apartment from Le Corbusier in 1931 and by the time it was completed, and de Beistigui came to decorate the interior, he had developed an interest in the style. In collaboration with architect-decorator Emilio Terry he created a surreal interior with out-of-scale furniture.

Ornate Second Empire gold-and-white chairs in the Cinema Room overpower the simple lines of Le Corbusier's spiral staircase, and on the roof terrace, artificial grass formed the carpet for baroque garden furniture. The walls were painted blue, and a mirror set above the fireplace reflected views of the Champs Elysées.

In the 1930s the influence of surrealism also affected France's leading interior decorator, Jean-Michel Frank (1895–1941), renowned for his supremely simple but expensively elegant interiors. He had influenced and supplied leading American

110

decorators, including Elsie de Wolfe, Frances Adler Elkins and
Eleanor Brown, with art deco emphasis on the quality and
rarity of the materials used. The Cinema Ballroom he designed
for Baron Roland de l'Espée (1936) was a major departure. The
colour scheme was startling: there was a bright red carpet and
one pink, one pale blue, one sea-green and one yellow wall.
The theatre boxes hung with purple velvet flanked the ultimate
in surrealist seating, the 'Mae West Lips' sofa (c. 1936) designed
by Dalí and based on his painting, *Mae West* (1934, Art Institute
of Chicago), which had depicted the film star's lips as a sofa,
her nose as a fireplace and her eyes as framed oil paintings.
The British versions were commissioned in deep and pale
pink felt by the great collector of surrealist art, Edward James,
for Monkton House near Chichester, the country home he
furnished and decorated as a monument to surrealism.
A series of strange room settings used quilting on the walls,
and a stair carpet was specially woven to reproduce James's
dog's pawprints.

Edward James also commissioned the painter Paul Nash
(1889–1946) to design a bathroom for his wife, the Viennese
dancer Tilly Losch, at his London house. Like many artists
during the Depression, Nash was forced to take on design work
in order to make a living. He wrote passionately on the subject
of design in his *Room and Book* (1932), decrying the British

111 Jean-Michel Frank: Cinema Ballroom for Baron Roland de l'Espée, Paris, 1936,
with the 'Mae West's Lips' sofa designed by Salvador Dalí.

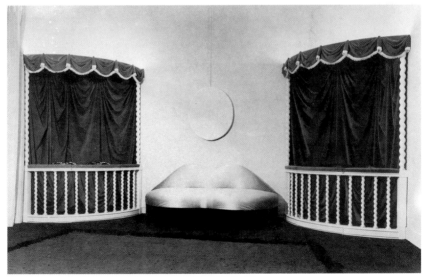

112 Paul Nash: all-glass bathroom for Tilly Losch, London, 1932. A painter's sleek
interior with stippled and plain mirror-glass.

taste for historical revivals: 'It is time we woke up and took an interest in our times. Just as the modern Italian has revolted against the idea that his country is nothing but a museum, so we should be ashamed to be regarded by the Americans as a charming old-world village.' In Tilly Losch's bathroom he provided a sleek interior with modern reflective materials. The walls were stippled glass, coated with an alloy to give a purple sheen, set off by peach-tinted mirrors. The fittings were all black, and the floor was covered in pink rubber. The fluorescent light on the wall was shaped as two half-moons, and the fitted electric fire was unusual enough at this time to be made a feature of the moderne interior. The moon was a recurring motif in Nash's paintings, and the chromed barre was inspired by the metaphysical cover he designed for the book *Dark Weeping* (1929).

American interior decorators were similarly influenced by the surrealist movement. Dorothy Draper (1889–1969) displayed her debt to surrealism in the dramatic use of scale and striking manipulation of expectations of inside/outside. At the Arrowhead Springs Hotel in Southern California (1935) she installed overscaled furniture and neo-baroque white plaster decorations, while at the Hampshire House Hotel, Central Park South, New York (1937), she designed the function rooms as an outdoor space, complete with garden furniture and the exterior of a Georgian house to unnerve the visitor. The flamboyant Rose Cumming (1887–1968) found the 'Old French taste' of women like McClelland or McMillen Brown stale, and combined raw silk, satin, metallic wallpaper and silver furniture in fantasy interiors inspired by surrealism and Hollywood cinema.

Cumming was of the same generation as de Wolfe, Ruby Ross Wood and Dorothy Draper. These women had pioneered the profession of interior decoration but were untrained; and brought with them an air of the dilettante. By the 1930s the whole profession had become more formalized. The American Institute of Interior Decorators (now the American Society of Interior Designers) was established in 1931, and trade magazines were founded in America including *Home Furnishing* from 1929 and *The Decorators' Digest* in 1932 (renamed *Interior Design* in the 1950s). A new generation entered the profession in the 1930s with more formal training in design and a more business-like approach. Terence Harold Robsjohn-Gibbings (1905–1976), for instance, had an architectural training. He was brought to America by Charles Duveen, the antique dealer and brother of art dealer Joseph Duveen, and set up his own practice on Madison Avenue, New York City, in 1936. His designs were inspired by Ancient Greece and the moderne.

113 TOP Dorothy Draper: room for the Quitandinha Hotel, Petropolis, near Rio de Janeiro, Brazil, 1946. Sweeping curves and oversized candelabra owe a debt to the baroque and surrealism.
114 ABOVE Rose Cumming: bedroom, the decorator's own apartment, New York, 1946. A luminous grand design of shimmering greys, mixing fine period furniture with oriental and fantasy elements.

The Klismos Chair and his mosaic-floored showroom (1936) display his eclectic knowledge of ancient and modern sources. His subsequent work for the California jeweller, Paul Flato, and his furniture designs indicate a debt to Swedish modernism. Less stark, with its extensive use of blond woods and other natural materials, Swedish modern was regarded as acceptable by the decorating world when the international modern was not. William Pahlmann (1900–1987) trained at the New York School of Fine and Applied Arts, and designed room settings for the New York department store Lord and Taylor from 1936. He promoted a variety of styles, including the moderne, as well as creating baroque settings worthy of the film *Gone With the Wind.*

The rise in status of the interior decorator was halted for a time after the Second World War by shortages, and then aided by the emergence of the new profession of 'interior designer'. Entrants to the profession would now usually be trained, relying less on 'natural good taste' and more on graduate education. Such designers increasingly worked on non-domestic commissions, as the commercial sector realized the value of good interior design.

In the grand milieu, John Fowler was succeeded as principal adviser to the National Trust in Britain in 1969 by David Mlinaric, who did not aim for the faded elegance of Fowler, but recreated period interiors with new textiles and gilding. Mlinaric's private commissions reveal an eclectic use of antiques from different centuries. Another new figure on the post-war decorating scene, Michael Inchbald (1920–2013), showed the same disregard for historical accuracy, and incorporated a varied mixture of past styles in his interiors. He designed the luxury interior of the *Queen Elizabeth 2* ocean liner, and his own London home provided a slightly quirky setting for an important collection of antique furniture and *objets d'art.* Perhaps the best known of all British interior decorators and designers, David Hicks (1929–1998), was an admirer of Inchbald's work, and he showed the same skill in combining antiques with modern design.

Hicks's career was launched in 1954 when the decoration of the interior of his mother's house in London was published in *House and Garden.* The combination of strong colours such as scarlet, black and cerulean blue in the library, the emphasis on crisp outline, and the careful table-top arrangements or 'tablescapes', all characterize Hick's work. After a four-year partnership with Tom Parr, who went on to run Colefax & Fowler, he established his own business, David Hicks Ltd, in 1959. During the 1960s he contributed to the renaissance

115 LEFT David Hicks: drawing room, Eaton Place, London, 1954. Bold combinations of strong colours used for the project that launched Hicks's career.
116 BELOW David Hicks: an artful division of bathroom and dressing-room, late 1960s. Note the geometric patterned rug.
117 OPPOSITE Billy Baldwin: dining room of apartment of Placido Arango in Madrid. A characteristic blend of old and new, including an El Greco original and Louis XVI gilt chairs; pale yellow walls and white curtains complement a geometrically patterned rug.

in British culture at a time when British pop groups,
fashion designers, photographers and models dominated
the international scene. His photograph appeared in *David
Bailey's Box of Pin-Ups* in 1965 as one of the young fashion
leaders working in London.

The bathroom he designed for his wife in their house in
the South of France in the late 1960s is characteristic of his
style, with white-painted furniture, louvred shutters and a bold
black-and-white patterned rug. The curtained bath ingeniously
divides the bathroom from the dressing room. For his own
Palladian Revival villa in Portugal in the 1980s, Hicks acted
as architect, designer and decorator.

Hicks's work, particularly his bold, geometric carpet and
fabric designs, was influential in the United States. The leading
post-war American interior decorator, Billy Baldwin (1903–1983),
wrote that Hicks had 'revolutionized the floors of the world
with his small-patterned and striped carpeting'. Baldwin
also excelled in blending antiques into modern interiors:
the 'Old French' style and Colonial Revival both remained
popular with American decorators. Baldwin had begun his
career working for Ruby Ross Wood in 1935, collaborating on
the surrealist interior for a house in Montego Bay, Jamaica,

117

in 1938. After Wood died in 1950 he went into partnership with designer Edward Martin in 1952. His debt to Wood is clear in his use of antiques in simple settings of plain white walls, bare floorboards and rush matting. Inspired by the brilliantly coloured paintings of Henri Matisse, he introduced exotic fabric prints and vivid mixtures of colours into his interiors during the 1950s. In the 1960s he became the most sought-after decorator in the USA, designing interiors for prominent figures such as the Paul Mellons and American *Vogue* editor and doyenne of fashion Diana Vreeland. His memoirs, *Billy Baldwin, An Autobiography* (1985), acknowledge his debt to the female pioneers of decorating, particularly Ruby Ross Wood.

Michael Taylor (1927–1986), who had a successful practice in San Francisco from 1957, was influenced by Syrie Maugham, acquiring most of Elkins's business estate when she died, including designs brought from Maugham. Albert Hadley (1920–2012) was an admirer of Eleanor Brown, and in 1956 joined McMillen Inc. as a decorator. He used lighting designed by De Wolfe in his own apartment in the late 1950s. In 1962 Hadley went into partnership with Mrs Henry Parish II, another woman decorator of the early generation who was then working on the refurbishment of the White House, Washington, DC, for President and Mrs Kennedy. The new interiors reflected the eighteenth-century classical origins of the building, and expressed Mrs Kennedy's interest in high culture. The firm of Parish-Hadley completed many historically based interiors during the 1970s. Post-war interior decorators have found lasting inspiration in the working practices of the women who founded the profession.

Chapter 6
Post-war Modernism

During and after the Second World War mainstream modernism was nurtured and developed in America. For the first time in the history of interior design, America led and Europe followed. The widespread feeling of hope and faith in the democratic ideal that characterized the early post-war years was expressed in the adoption of modernism in all areas of design. It had connotations of egalitarianism, dynamism and technological expertise.

Among the chief modern architects of the first generation now living and working in America, Mies van der Rohe had left Germany in 1938 to become Professor of Architecture at the Amour (now Illinois) Institute of Technology. He designed a complete new campus for the college in a crisply efficient style using exposed-steel frames and brick-and-glass infills. He also undertook domestic commissions on the same principles, such as the house he designed in 1950 for Dr Edith Farnsworth near Chicago. This consists of a rectangular terrace with steps leading up to a single-storey rectangular living area. There are no rooms as such. Areas for different functions are delimited by storage units that do not quite reach the ceiling. The simple steel framework of the building is sheathed in plate glass and metal screening to create a feeling of openness and interaction with nature that was to inspire countless post-war interiors.

With Mies's Seagram Building, New York, we see modernism adopted as the appropriate progressive image for multinational corporations. American firms such as the huge architectural practice of Skidmore, Owings and Merrill had offices worldwide and an army of draughtsmen to design modern skyscrapers. Gordon Bunshaft (1909–1990) of SOM designed the definitive high-rise block with Lever House, New York (1950–2), for the multinational corporation Lever Brothers. The curtain-walled slab rises from a mezzanine floor on *pilotis.* Many of the technical innovations that characterized post-war interior design are already exploited in the interior. The suspended ceiling of each floor screens services such as air-conditioning and electric cables, which became more readily accessible for maintenance than when concealed below floorboards or behind plaster. The interior working space was opened up, with rows of desks and small dividing screens replacing corridors and small office rooms.

The Quickborner Team, a German management consultancy, developed the concept of an open office during the 1950s, with huge floors broken up by fabric-covered screens, desks, filing cabinets and plants. The layout is designed around the traffic flow rather than rigidly defining work hierarchies. This system has now been adopted worldwide, although by the 1970s the suitability of such purely functional and controlled working environments was being questioned, as the performance of office workers came under close scrutiny.

The Union Carbide Headquarters in New York City by SOM (1959) had a worldwide influence. The multi-storey block was conceived as a system of co-ordinated parts, with an understated but expensive exterior of glass curtain-walls with stainless-steel extrusions. The interior partitions, filing cabinets and grid on the ceiling echo the pattern of the rectangular window mullions. The working environment is totally controlled, with air-conditioning and an illuminated ceiling. Hierarchies within the firm are symbolized chiefly by seating, with management occupying the top storeys and places beside the windows, but also by the size of the work station and amount of privacy. This was the first office block to be fully carpeted in order to cut down noise.

Such innovations marked the rise of so-called contract interiors, that is, interiors designed for commercial as opposed to domestic use. SOM established themselves as world leaders of this market, providing multi-storey office blocks for Pepsi Cola and the Chase Manhattan Bank during the early 1960s. The style of the interiors, under the direction of Davis Allen (1916–1999), remained conventionally modern, generally a less lavish version of Mies van der Rohe's characteristic style.

Before joining SOM Allen had worked for the Knoll Planning Unit. Under the direction of Florence Knoll, the Unit was the

118

119

118 OPPOSITE ABOVE Open plan design with ordered rows of 'work stations'.
119 OPPOSITE BELOW The perfect example of the commercial modern interior: Ward Bennett and Davis Allen of SOM, office for David Rockefeller, Chase Manhattan Bank, 1958–61. Bennett acquired works of art and designed the furniture.

120 Philip Johnson: living room, the 'Glass House', New Canaan, Connecticut, 1949. Glass, bare bricks and concrete make the carpet appear an island. Note the use of the Barcelona chair and stool.

major practice in America devoted solely to commercial interior design. As with SOM, the style used to symbolize American capitalism for CBS, H.J. Heinz and Cowles Magazines was inspired mainly by the minimal but prestigious and expensive work of Mies van der Rohe.

In the domestic area, the crusade to educate the public about modern design had been carried on by the Museum of Modern Art, New York, from its foundation in 1931. The book *What Is Modern Interior Design?* published in 1953, grew out of an exhibition, 'Modern Rooms of the Last Fifty Years', in 1947. The curator, Edgar Kauffman, traced the evolution of the modern interior from William Morris via the Bauhaus, culminating with Frank Lloyd Wright. All the examples listed are by architects, and are of privately commissioned houses, or exhibitions.

Mies's foremost disciple Philip Johnson (1906–2005), who had been responsible for bringing the International Style to America with the 1932 exhibition at the Museum of Modern Art, designed his own house at New Canaan (1949), labelled

120

144   Chapter 6

the 'Glass House', as a simple cube with four glass curtain-walls. The integration of inside and outside is complete.

Alexander Girard (1907–1993) was one of the new post-war architect-designers who specialized in modern interiors. He underwent architectural training in Paris, Florence, Rome, London and New York, before establishing his own practice in the Detroit area to work for large corporations such as the Ford Motor Company (1943), Lincoln Motors (1946), and, from 1953, as fabrics designer for Herman Miller. His domestic interior designs are typical of the post-war modern movement in America. The Rieveschel House at Grosse Pointe Farms, Michigan (1952), and his own house of 1948 in the same area have built-in furniture, screens, and Corbusian ramps linking rooms. The 'natural' element is introduced with fur rugs on the floors, indoor plants, and the use of natural light wherever possible. An atmosphere of light, spaciousness and natural forms also characterizes the work of the architect-designer William Lescaze (1896–1969), who had brought European

121

121 Alexander Girard: living room, Rieveschel House, Grosse Pointe Farms, Michigan, 1952. A compendium of the elements of the International modern style.

modernism to America when he emigrated from Switzerland before the war. The living room of the Norman House, New York City (1941), has a plain carpet and furnishing fabrics, floor-to-ceiling fenestration, plants, and chairs designed by Alvar Aalto that attest to the continuing influence of Scandinavian modern.

Russel Wright (1904–1976) was one of the few Americans to design modern interiors without an architectural training. His background was in fine art, and he progressed through theatre design to industrial design in the late 1920s, when he began to design ceramic tableware, including the highly influential 'American Modern' in 1937. This was included in the first Museum of Modern Art 'Good Design' show in 1949, and remained in production until 1959. He experimented with new materials such as spun aluminium, melamine, vinyl and metals in the design of functional objects such as a chair with a concealed writing table and magazine rack, and oven-to-table ware. Despite his interest in new materials, his interiors were

122 BELOW Harwell Hamilton Harris: Havens House, Berkeley, California, 1941. The 'Bay Region' style, using wooden panelling and Aalto-inspired chairs
123 OPPOSITE LEFT Le Corbusier: double-storey living room, Unité d'Habitation, Marseilles, 1952.
124 OPPOSITE RIGHT Le Corbusier: Maisons Jaoul, Neuilly, 1956. Curves are introduced, and exposed brickwork and concrete are used as elements of interior design.

marked by the modernist integration of interior and exterior. At his own duplex in New York City the paving slabs of the garden continue into the living area to provide continuity.

In California, where the climate favours integrating the interior and outdoors, George Home, Harwell Hamilton Harris and Richard Neutra used huge expanses of glass that unified the living and terrace areas. The living room of the Havens House by Harris has wooden panelling – a common feature of the West Coast interior, as wood is cheaply available locally – rush matting, floor-to-ceiling windows, built-in furniture and Aalto chairs.

Such mainstream modern interiors reflect developments in Europe inspired by the third leading figure of the International Style (with Mies and Gropius), Le Corbusier. After the war Le Corbusier remained in France but designed complete buildings as far away as India, where he had complete control over the new capital for the state of Punjab, Chandigarh, in the 1950s. In France he designed a mass dwelling unit, the Unité d'Habitation at Marseilles (1952), as the realization of his theories about housing a whole community in a self-contained

122

123

125 Frank Lloyd Wright: Solomon R. Guggenheim Museum, New York City, 1959. The exhibition area consists of one gently spiralling ramp.

multi-storey slab. Communal facilities were sited on the roof, and one floor was devoted to shops. The plan allowed for a double-storey living room and balcony for each flat. Le Corbusier's influence was also paramount for the individual domestic interior, notably with his decision to leave internal brickwork and concrete exposed in the Maisons Jaoul at Neuilly (1956).

Le Corbusier's other great contribution to post-war modern interior design was to create a more organic modernism with the Nôtre-Dame-du-Haut chapel at Ronchamp, Haute-Saône (1955). The parabolic shape of the building is highly sculptural in comparison with the clean geometric lines of his pre-war work. Inside the chapel, the thick concrete walls are pierced by small coloured windows to create the dramatic effect of shafts of coloured light falling on the congregation.

Frank Lloyd Wright was also working in a much more organic and sculptural way in the post-war era. The interior of the Solomon R. Guggenheim Museum (1959) on Fifth Avenue, New York, consists of a single spiralling ramp that makes up the main exhibition space.

124

125

The new interest in curved organic forms can also be seen in the work of Eero Saarinen (1910–1961), whose TWA terminal at JFK International Airport, New York (1962), is based on the outspread wings of an insect in flight.

Leading American furniture designers too were inspired by organic, amoeboid forms. The curved forms of the new furniture were first seen at the Museum of Modern Art in 1940 as part of the 'Organic Design in Home Furnishings' competition. Designers trained at the Cranbrook Academy in Bloomfield Hills, Michigan, were now producing furniture that challenged European dominance. Founded in 1932 and managed by the Finnish architect Eliel Saarinen, Cranbrook trained a whole generation of important designers, including Charles and Ray Eames, Eero Saarinen and Harry Bertoia who

126 Eero Saarinen: TWA terminal (now Terminal 5), JFK International Airport, New York, 1962. Softly curving lines supersede the harsh geometric forms of pre-war modernism

127-30 Charles Eames's shell chair, 1951 (top left), and stacking chairs, 1955 (above right). Above left: Eero Saarinen's Pedestal chair abolishes the clutter of chair legs. Opposite: The living room of the Case Study House No. 20, Altadena, California, 1958, furnished with Saarinen's Womb chair (left) and Pedestal chair and table (background).

came to the forefront in the 1950s. Inspired by a modern but humanist aesthetic, the Cranbrook designers regarded mass production in a positive light as bringing 'good design' to the mass market.

New techniques for moulding and glueing plywood had been discovered by American manufacturers during wartime production for the Navy and were now exploited for furniture design, as were plastics with fibre-glass reinforcements. The first chair to be mass produced in plastic was Charles Eames's shell chair, which had a single moulded unit for seat and back, made of fibre-glass-reinforced polyester resin. Such chairs were light, durable and easy to store, and were much used for the burgeoning contract interior-design trade. The new materials and techniques were also perfect for Eames's and Saarinen's designs, which usually consisted of an ergonomically formed one-piece seating unit supported by tapered metal legs. Eero Saarinen's Womb chair (1946) and Pedestal furniture (1955) and Charles and Ray Eames's Chair and Ottoman (1956) are among the classics of twentieth-century chair-design.

127-8

129-30

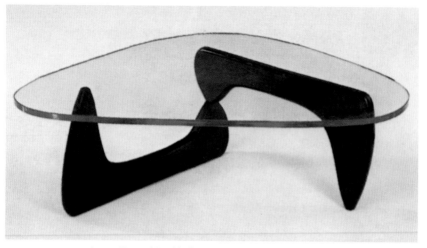

131 ABOVE Isamu Noguchi: table for Herman Miller, 1944. An early example of the organic forms of post-war modernism. Noguchi's inspiration was the art of Japan, where the sculptor had spent his childhood.
132 OPPOSITE Living room of the Eames's own house, Santa Monica, California, 1948.

Such pieces were mass produced by two leading American manufacturers of modern furniture: the Knoll Furniture Company and Herman Miller. Knoll had been founded in 1938. A graduate of Cranbrook, Florence Schust had married Hans Knoll and established the Knoll Planning Unit for interior design in 1946. The Unit was responsible mainly for contract interiors based on the Miesian aesthetic of simple, geometric, but expensive finishes. The Furniture Company manufactured Mies's Barcelona chair from 1948, and it was used in the furnishing of such interiors. Knoll also manufactured Harry Bertoia's wire-mesh Diamond chair (1952), and Saarinen's Womb chair and Pedestal furniture. Herman Miller Inc. mass produced leading examples of modern furniture designed

131 by sculptors, including Isamu Noguchi's important design for a palette-shaped glass-topped table in 1944. Their leading designs by Charles and Ray Eames included plastic shell chairs on metal legs, all-wire chairs, stacking chairs in plastic, and the influential bent-plywood chair and ottoman with black leather upholstery of 1956. Herman Miller also manufactured new types of furniture for storage, including George Nelson's 'Basic Storage Components' (1949), which consisted of open shelving, drawers, a cupboard and a desk, and could replace

132 a non-supporting wall. The Eames's own house-studio at Santa Monica was constructed from industrial components such as open-webbed steel joists and pre-fabricated steel

133 Gio Ponti: living room, Appartamento Luccano, Milan, 1950. Boldly mixed patterns of manufacturers' labels on the curtains and witty *trompe l'œil* bookshelves and 'woodgrain' on walls and upholstery.

decking, and provided an appropriately modern setting for their furniture designs.

American design reached Europe mainly by way of magazines. *Domus,* for example, brought it to Italy, where it had a great impact on that war-ravaged country. Supported by generous American funding, the Italian government was endeavouring to foster a new national spirit based on liberal democracy. The strict lines of the modern movement were associated with pre-war fascism, and the curved, organic inspiration was a welcome alternative. Italian design of the post-war era was also heavily influenced by avant-garde art, particularly the sculpture of Henry Moore and Alexander Calder.

Gio Ponti (1891–1979), founder and editor of *Domus* from 1947, was one of the designers who embraced American modernism, mixing it with the rich inheritance of the Italian decorative arts. His interiors were frequently decorated with *trompe l'oeil* paintings, or with upholstery that recalls the coloured-marble tables produced for eighteenth-century visitors on the Grand

133

Tour. As America had Knoll and Herman Miller to encourage modern design, Italy had Cassina, which manufactured work by Gio Ponti, Vico Magistretti and Mario Bellini for the all-important export market. One of the first projects was the 'Superleggera' side-chair by Gio Ponti (1956), which had a spiky black frame and white woven seat inspired by traditional fishermen's chairs. In Turin, a circle of designers led by Carlo Mollino designed surrealist interiors.

In France, the same correlation was made between democratic ideals and modernism. The country had been devastated by the war, and the 1940s and 1950s were spent in rebuilding bombed cities. Nevertheless, there was a new spirit in French design, which absorbed American influence just as French New Wave film directors revered American films. The modern architect Jean Prouvé (1901–1984) showed a dining-room setting in 1948 with tapered-leg furniture in a style similar to the work of the Cranbrook Academy. It was typical in using the traditional material, wood, and in moving towards a more organic form of modernism. French decorators such as Madeleine Castaing, Jules Lelue and Dominique clung to past

134

134 Jean Prouvé: dining room, 1948. An example of French post-war modern interior design. Before the war the modern architect Prouvé had specialized in steel construction.

135 British Utility furniture on display at the Building Centre, London, 1942. Utility launched official 'good taste' in wartime Britain.

135

traditions, and it was not until the 1960s that French design welcomed innovation, with the impact of pop.

The British government officially adopted modernism during the war with the Utility scheme. Britain's total involvement in the war effort had left a shortage of materials and labour for furniture and furnishings. The Board of Trade could not call a complete halt to the manufacture of such items, as the needs of newly married couples and families who had lost their homes in bombing raids had somehow to be met. Furniture was allocated on a points system, according to need. Prices were fixed by the government, and, more significantly for the history of interior design, so were styling and materials.

The Council for Art and Industry's 1937 report on 'The Working Class Home, its Furnishings and Equipment' had deplored the taste for surface ornament and period revivals. The Council's Committee defined good design as 'items in which the design was simple, of good proportions and without dust-collecting features', and stressed the importance of 'good construction'. This definition was shared by the Advisory Committee, who managed the introduction of the Utility scheme in 1942. The designer and manufacturer Gordon Russell, who headed the special Design Panel, welcomed the

156   Chapter 6

opportunity to influence mass taste, writing in 1946: 'I felt that to raise the whole standard of furniture for the mass of the people was not a bad war job.' Middle-class notions of 'good taste' were imposed on a public with no choice but to buy Utility.

The names of ranges such as 'Chiltern' and 'Cotswold' of 1946 reveal Russell's continued loyalty to the arts and crafts movement. The furniture was well made, sensible and solid, with traditional features such as the ladderback for chairs. The simplicity of the designs could also be traced to Russell's admiration for Swedish modern. The scheme was phased out soon after the war, and by 1948 the Utility mark denoted only a certain quality and a controlled price. Manufacturers were again free to produce their own designs, within loose guidelines, and the public demand for ornament and period features, particularly Tudor, could once more be met.

British officials and supporters of modern design were encouraged by the supposed success of the Utility scheme, and a Council of Industrial Design was established to encourage good design in 1945. The first public manifestation of the CoID was an exhibition organized at the Victoria and Albert Museum entitled 'Britain Can Make It'. Visitors flocked to see the show, which included room-settings for various consumers ranging on the social scale from coal-miner to television broadcaster. In a Mass Observation Survey visitors criticized the sobriety of many of the exhibits, which recalled Utility, a style the majority had found uninspiring. Russell continued his campaign for good design as Chairman of the CoID during the 1950s.

But what of the design of the interiors which Utility furnished? Official exhibitions favoured the 'folksy' touch, with simple gingham check curtains and plain white walls. Simplicity was enforced by shortages. As the *Home Book* of 1950 advised: 'There is only a limited choice for wall treatments at the present time, and most people have to be content with distempering, but as conditions improve so the choice will widen to include paint, enamel, paper, wood panelling and probably new finishes of various kinds.'

An architectural movement in Britain, the New Brutalists, was inspired by Le Corbusier. Its leading members, Alison and Peter Smithson, designed Hunstanton School, Norfolk (1954), making full use of the pre-fabricated elements of construction within the buildings as an aesthetic feature. Another prominent member of the group, James Stirling, designed the flats at Ham Common, London (1958), with the frank exposure of brickwork and concrete that he had seen at the Maisons Jaoul at Neuilly.

During the 1950s the speed and ease of inter-continental travel and the proliferation of media like films and television

136 Architect-designed living room for a London flat, a mainstream example of the 1950s interior. From Noel Carrington, *Colour and Pattern in the Home,* London, 1954.

disseminated the American modern look throughout the world. The typical American modern interior shared certain motifs with its European counterparts, whether in France, Germany, Italy, Spain or Holland. These included indoor plants, built-in furniture, animal skins as floor coverings, narrow venetian blinds, open storage space in the main living area and smooth, organic forms. There was a tendency to juxtapose textures and patterns. The seating often consisted of amoeboid units supported on thin black metal legs. Lighting was another key aspect of the international modern interior. A scattering of free-standing lamps superseded wall-brackets or the single source of light fixed to the ceiling. A house by the Architects Co-Partnership in Hampstead, London, of 1956 makes use of all these features, and integrates garden and living space with a sliding glass door leading to a balcony.

The international mainstream modern style of interior design had been established by architects trained in the International Style. The interior designer as such had yet to emerge. As late as 1967, Hugh Casson, the architect-designer and founder of the first post-graduate course at the Royal College of Art in London, commented that 'Many architects refuse to believe that such a thing as interior design exists at all. Some place it on a par with the art of the milliner or pastry cook; others seem to regard its claims for separate consideration as a personal affront.'

Other areas of design had become the preserve of the expert since the war. Commercial artists were now graphic designers, and the industrial designer enjoyed an improved status. The failure of interior design to match these areas in terms of professionalism harks back to its foundation by decorators. The Incorporated Institute of British Decorators, founded in 1889 by leading craftsmen, added the words 'and Interior Designers' to its title in 1953, recognizing that a new area of expertise had emerged. Then, in 1976, the word 'decorator' was dropped, and the organization became the British Institute of Interior Design. In 1987 it merged with the Chartered Society of Designers. The parallel American institutions followed a similar path. The American Institute of Interior Decorators, founded in 1931, became the American Society for Interior Designers in the 1970s. Magazines followed the same lines, with the American periodical *Interior Design and Decoration,* published for the interior designer from 1937, dropping the word 'decoration' from the title in the 1950s, and *The Interior Decorator* becoming simply *Interiors* in 1940. Professional journals were late emerging in Britain, and did not follow the American lead. New interiors were featured intermittently in established architectural magazines like *Architectural Review,* founded in 1896. *The World of Interiors,* devoted to domestic design, first appeared in November 1981, and *Designers' Journal,* Britain's foremost contract interior design magazine, only in 1983.

In Britain, the profession of interior designer became formalized in the late 1960s with the inauguration of tertiary-level courses. By 1968 five art colleges ran diploma courses for interior designers, and the Royal College of Art's School of Interior Design had instituted a post-graduate course. In the United States, the Parsons School of Design, New York, founded by Charles Alvah Parsons, specialized in interior design training as early as 1896, and was followed by the New York School of Interior Design in 1916 and the Fashion Institute of Technology, New York, in 1951. By the 1980s the majority of American art colleges offered degrees in interior design.

With interior design training established, the next hurdle was to gain the respect of architects. This could only happen when modern movement tenets, that the architect should be responsible for the total building and that form should follow function, were called into question with post-modernism. The process began during the 1950s with the explosion of consumerism and the emergence of a pop aesthetic.

Chapter 7
Consumer Culture

A consumer boom, beginning in the 1950s in America and spreading throughout Europe in the 1960s, had a profound effect on the taste-making process in interior design. For the design of the domestic interior, initiative passed from the architect and interior decorator to the consumer, who now exercised a greater degree of choice than ever before, right across the social spectrum.

In the American decorating manual *The Complete Book of Interior Decorating* (1956), home journalists Mary Derieux and Isabelle Stevenson advised the reader to: 'Start an indexed scrapbook in which you can collect magazine articles, advertisements of new types of equipment and furnishings, room pictures and color schemes which appeal to you.' For the first time it was stressed: 'Don't be afraid to give expression to your own taste in making your selections. It is *your* home.'

The tradition of home advice manuals for the middle-class woman had been established in the nineteenth century. Guidance on taste could also be gleaned from a wealth of writings by designers and critics of all kinds. However, such books generally recommended one style only and criticized all other trends. In 1954 Donald D. MacMillan was advising in *Good Taste in Home Decoration* that '... the accepted standards of good taste in the field of interior design have developed over a long stretch of time and a knowledge of these standards is invaluable'. Interior decorators who were won over by the moderne during the inter-war years advocated this over all other styles. Propagandists of the modern movement tried to influence public taste through the DIA yearbooks in Britain, and in America with Museum of Modern Art exhibitions and associated pamphlets. The authority of such tastemakers was eroded during the 1950s, and the question of what constituted 'good' taste became confused.

In America, huge suburban sites were developed to cater for a booming middle-class population. The American family moved house more frequently than its pre-war predecessor, and needed to communicate important statements about itself and its place in a particular social milieu through the appearance of the home. The home was re-established as the province of the wife. The role of the housewife had shifted dramatically as a result of the Second World War. During the war, women in America and Britain were officially encouraged to enter the factories and take on traditionally male jobs, for example as riveters, welders and turners. A 'make do and mend' approach was adopted in the home. After the war, men returning from the fighting needed jobs, and the importance of the domestic role of women was reasserted by the mass media and the authorities. Dior's New Look of 1946 reinforced a traditional role for women with its emphasis on the bust, waist and hips and unpractical stiletto heels, and the woman's traditional job as mother and housekeeper was given greater emphasis through scientific justification. A new image of the professional housewife was constructed by the media.

The housewife became an important target for the advertiser and manufacturer as soon as it was realized that she was responsible for handling the family budget. As David Riesman observed in his survey of American consumerism, *The Lonely Crowd* (1950), 'women are the accepted leaders of consumption in our society'. This factor was important for the development of kitchen design in the post-war years. New domestic gadgets such as the electric food-mixer, toaster and kettle were accommodated in larger kitchens, with ample storage space provided by fitted units, laminated with coloured and patterned plastics. Double cookers, fridges and washing machines grew larger in America, and began to appear in British homes for the first time. The large size of such items was not functionally necessary. The design of fridges was based on car design, being streamlined, and they came in colours such as salmon-pink or turquoise with chromium trim. Manufacturers had realized the importance of design obsolescence, and the status-conscious housewife needed to be persuaded that she wanted the latest style with 'added extras'. The servantless kitchen was no longer out-of-bounds to family and callers and needed to impress the guest. This development marked a reversal of the scientific approach of the 1930s, when kitchens were made as small as possible, being based on the ship's galley. Now the American kitchen

137-8

137–41 Consumerism expressed by large kitchens surfaced with brightly coloured plastic laminates, streamlined fridges, freezers, the informal breakfast bar and the family games room, and not least the family automobile.

provided the main focus of the domestic interior, signifying that the woman of the house was always there, that her domestic duties were paramount.

The open-plan arrangement that was popularized by modern architects during the 1950s made the kitchen an integral part of the ground-floor living area. The living area in these new houses was larger than the pre-war equivalent, for it frequently incorporated a dining area with a 'breakfast bar' to divide it from the kitchen. There was interest in dual-purpose rooms.

The seating inspired by the designs of the Cranbrook Academy would now be arranged around the television set, rather than facing the fire as previously. Heating was provided by radiators, allowing a flexible furniture arrangement. Strong colours such as lime-green and orange contrasted with black were fashionable, as were standard lamps, low, boomerang-shaped tables of metal and plastic laminate, and indoor plants. The exuberance of the new consumer guaranteed a heterogeneous mixture of styles. As well as modern, 'Old French', Colonial and Spanish Mission styles remained popular.

Post-war prosperity and growth also brought a revolution in shopping habits and transport. Huge supermarkets were built on the edges of towns, as were drive-in cafes and cinemas, reflecting the fact that America had become a car-owning nation. The interiors of these vehicles were designed with fantasy, not function in mind. Like the contemporary kitchens, they were much larger than function demanded, with generous upholstery, and wraparound windscreens and chromed control instruments largely based on popular science fiction imagery, as exemplified in the 1954 Cadillac and 1957 Chevrolet Bel Air. The interiors of jet airliners, another important new mode of transport, were more stringently controlled by space,

142

142 Harley Earl: Cadillac interior, 1954. The styling of wheel, chrome air-vents, levers and dials owes more to science fiction and aeroplane design than to function.

dimensions and ergonomics. Harley Earl (1893–1969), the head of design at General Motors from 1927 to 1959, also worked as an interior designer, and when he designed the interior of the General Dynamics Convair 880, he tried to break up the monotony of the long narrow interior by making a break in the ceiling fitting on every fifth row. Foam shells formed the seating, which was crisply upholstered in blue. A scarlet aisle-carpet and white gold-flecked fabric covering the walls and ceiling provided a decorative effect.

The interiors of diners and bars were flamboyant, with pastel-coloured plastic seats and laminated, built-in tables with chrome fittings, in the organic shapes of post-war modernism.

The development of popular American design during the late 1940s and 1950s horrified the British design establishment who were attempting to promote a more functional style. Concerned about the continuing taste for revivals, the Council of Industrial Design launched a successful campaign to promote a new style: the Contemporary.

The most significant vehicle for the campaign was the Festival of Britain, held in 1951. This was a patriotic celebration of the past, present and future achievements of Great Britain on the centenary of the Great Exhibition of 1851. The Contemporary Style was launched by the CoID in its magazine for industry and the consumer, *Design,* in February 1949. The Council invited manufacturers to submit exhibits for the Festival which should be 'lively and of today, which does not exclude those basic designs that remain as good as they have ever been, such as the Windsor chair and many hand-tools'.

Thus the Contemporary Style provided an effective blend of the latest developments in American and Swedish design with British traditions. The Contemporary Style was first seen by the public at the Festival site, where the CoID mounted an exhibition of room settings and launched the Design Index, enabling the public to browse through examples of 'good design' mounted on cards.

143-4   The interiors and furniture designed for the Festival site were all vetted by the Council and typify the Contemporary Style. Chairs designed by Ernest Race and Robin Day are skeletal constructions with great stress placed on line. They are simple in that they have no surface decoration, and they have splayed legs, a feature common to all Contemporary furniture and inspired by Cranbrook designs of the 1940s. The thin chair legs rest on balls, another key feature of Contemporary-style furniture. This motif derived from the CoID's introduction of the theme of molecular biology for the Festival Pattern Group. The Group consisted of twenty-eight British manufacturers

143-4 'Contemporary' living room, Council of Industrial Design, 1951, below. Officially approved British design, exhibited at the Festival of Britain in 1951. Left, Ernest Race's Antelope chair, designed for use throughout the Festival site.

who based textile prints, light fittings, glass and ceramics on diagrams of crystal structures: for example, the fabric 'Helmsley' designed by Marianne Straub for Warner and Sons Ltd was based on the chemical structure of nylon.

The whimsical and decorative nature of the Contemporary Style ensured its success with the consumer. This was in no small part also due to the sustained propaganda campaign instigated by the CoID after the Festival, using women's magazines, television and exhibitions to put the message over to the public. Each year at the *Daily Mail* Ideal Home Exhibition the CoID mounted a display of room settings which, it felt, represented that year's norm of good interior design. In 1955, in the sixth of these displays, the Council furnished a flat designed by Robert and Margery Westmore in the Contemporary Style with furniture that could be bought at a high street retailer, in this case Williams Furniture Galleries, Kilburn. Such schemes were aimed at the new occupants of local authority housing. Post-war public housing generally offered smaller living spaces than its pre-war equivalent, hence the lightweight, functional pieces of Contemporary furniture were popular and replaced more solid items such as the bulky three-piece suite of the 1930s. The open-plan layout of many flats and houses ensured the popularity of the room divider, which could separate the living from the dining area. George Nelson's upmarket prototype was manufactured in Britain by E. Gomme and Sons Ltd as part of its range of interchangeable unit furniture marketed as 'G-Plan' from 1953.

Many features of the Contemporary interior derived from architect-designed models. Natural elements such as indoor plants, simple varnished wood, bare brick and natural stone created an effect of lightness, airiness and functionalism. Desperately needed public housing was provided in Britain with various New Towns in order that the suburban sprawl of London and the other major cities should be halted. Crawley in Sussex was designated a New Town after the war and the show houses were furnished in the Contemporary style for working-class Londoners seeking a better quality of life away from the pollution and overcrowding of the capital.

Colour and pattern were also important features of the Contemporary interior. Wallpapers and fabrics were printed with pastel backgrounds and black linear patterns derived from modern sculpture or, for kitchens, with designs of fruits, vegetables or crockery. The Contemporary-style interior often featured the mixing and matching of very different patterns. This was encouraged by the home advice manuals, for example, in *Newnes Home Management* it was suggested that contrasting wallpapers of spots and stripes should be used to add interest to chimney-breasts. The do-it-yourself market originated in America and flourished in America and Britain during the 1950s, encouraged by the magazine *Do-It-Yourself,* founded in 1957. Texas Homecare in Britain, for example, began as a family business in 1911 manufacturing wooden fireplaces. In 1954 the company opened several shops selling wallpapers and paint. In 1972 the company opened the first warehouse for the large-scale provision of materials for home improvements; by the late 1980s there were nearly two hundred such retail outlets. The market for such goods for the non-professional decorator had partly been stimulated by comparatively simple-to-use emulsion paints and vinyl wallpapers.

The widespread popularity of the Contemporary ironically led to its demise. As the mass-market demand for splayed legged plastic-laminated coffee tables increased into the 1960s, so the interest of professional designers waned. Architects were dismissive of the Contemporary as a fashionable style, to be outlived by the permanent values of modernism.

By the early 1950s the monolithic laws of classic modernism were beginning to be called into question. Members of the Independent Group, which met sporadically at the Institute of Contemporary Arts in London from 1952 to 1955, dismissed

145 Young homemakers turn to do-it-yourself. Roller-printing with paint for contrasting patterns in pink and green.

146 Richard Hamilton's inventory of American consumerism: *Just What Is It That Makes Today's Homes So Different, So Appealing?*, 1956.

modernism as outdated. Leading members, including the design writer Reyner Banham, architects Alison and Peter Smithson and James Stirling, and artists Eduardo Paolozzi and Richard Hamilton formulated a new cultural critique based on their enthusiasm for popular American design. The Group was fascinated by the American way of life as represented by the lavish interiors seen in Hollywood films and colour advertisements in magazines such as *McCalls* and *National Geographic*. Well-stocked refrigerators, automatic washing machines and televisions had an obvious appeal in the austere economic climate of Britain in the early 1950s. This avarice can be seen in Richard Hamilton's *Just What Is It That Makes Today's Homes So Different, So Appealing?* (1956), an inventory of all the objects of mass consumption enjoyed in American homes.

146

Consumer Culture

147 Alison and Peter Smithson: 'House of the Future', Ideal Home Exhibition, 1956 (shown with the roof removed). Moulded room-components cluster round a central patio space.

147

Independent Group discussions inspired Alison and Peter Smithson to design a 'House of the Future' for the *Daily Mail* Ideal Home Exhibition of 1956, according to Reyner Banham based on the styling and marketing of American cars. The Smithsons' House was moulded in plastic in a range of colours with chromium trim, and was intended to be updated every year. Like many interiors of the 1950s, that of the house was open plan, with the function of each area defined by the built-in furniture and appliances. The House demonstrates the way in which technology was idolized during the 1950s as a means of liberating the housewife to allow her to spend more time with her family. The House created a great deal of media interest with its labour-saving devices, such as the portable electronic dust-collector, waste-disposal unit, dishwasher and gamma-ray machine for treating foods.

The Smithsons' major achievement was to design a piece of expendable architecture. Modern movement theorists had always preached the value of an everlasting style, linking modernism with the buildings of Ancient Greece. The Smithsons believed that architects should learn from mass culture, and apply the lessons of rapidly changing styles and popular appeal to architectural design.

In the late 1950s the 'expendable aesthetic' began to apply increasingly to interior design. Swiftly changing fashions were inspired by a whole range of sources, but notably, not by mainstream architecture. One crucial source for new interior design was a new type of consumer. In the 1950s there was the phenomenon of the teenager. The spending power of the sixteen- to twenty-four-year-old age group had risen meteorically since the mid-1950s as young people enjoyed full employment and reasonable wages. A report commissioned by a London advertising agency in 1959 estimated the spending power of the British teenage sector in the previous year to be £900 million. The result was a new market sector that needed to make a distinct cultural statement.

Previously young people had unquestioningly assumed the style of interior offered by their parents. Now young people demanded that their own territory should symbolize their new independence. This was commonly seen in the decoration of the teenager's bedroom within the parental home with posters, records and record player. In the 1950s the coffee bar provided a meeting place for the young in Britain. These were generally run by first-generation Italians and featured a chrome coffee machine prominently displayed on the counter. The best-known example of the espresso coffee machine was designed by Gio Ponti for Gaggia in 1949. As one of the Independent Group, Toni del Renzio, commented in 1957: 'The espresso is doubtless part of a strong Italian influence that includes the motor-scooter and a new line in movie heroines.' In London Douglas Fisher designed 'The Gondola' in Wigmore Street and the 'Mocamba' and 'El Cubano' on Brompton Road within this genre. Tables were usually covered in bright plastic laminate with aluminium trim, and the furniture was the popular Contemporary. An Alpine motif was often introduced, and walls were frequently faced in stone or decorated with stone-effect wallpaper.

The American influence was also powerful, with the totem of youth culture, the juke box, on display. Like many items of industrial design of the era in America, the 1950s Wurlitzers were based on the visual imagery of car design, with chromium plating, wrap-around screens, quasi-dashboard for selecting the records, and even red lights and tailfins. The affluence of American teenagers in comparison with those of Europe was marked by new drive-in fast-food outlets designed for the age group.

Design for the youth market exploded in the 1960s with even greater affluence and a new feeling of breaking down the barriers of conventional social mores. This was expressed in the pop design movement which first emerged in Britain

148 Biba, London, 1972. Art deco motifs and Victorian bentwood hat stands evoke an ambience of 'retro-chic' in Barbara Hulanicki's first Kensington High Street store.

as part of the general pop movement. In 1963 the Beatles had three number one hits in Britain, and their American tour in the following year established British dominance as world leader of youth culture. This manifested itself in interior design with the creation of new environments for the youth market, such as the boutique, a small shop selling inexpensive, trendy clothes exclusively for the young. The first, Bazaar, was opened by fashion designer Mary Quant (b. 1934) in King's Road, Chelsea, in 1955. She moved to a new shop in Knightsbridge in 1957, designed by Terence Conran (b. 1931), featuring a central staircase with the clothes hanging beneath, and bales of fabric decorating the upper parts of the interior. By the mid-1960s these small shops had opened in cities throughout Britain.

148
In 1964 Barbara Hulanicki (b. 1936) opened the first Biba shop off Kensington High Street in London. The interior was dimly lit and pop music played loudly the whole time. The walls and floor of the Biba stores that followed were decorated in dark tones, the clothes hung on bentwood Victorian hat stands, and ostrich feathers in nineteenth-century vases added to the decadent atmosphere.

The need for young people to dissociate themselves from the older generation and communicate fun and transience explains the diverse inspirations for pop. The decorative styles of the past were revived, particularly art nouveau after an exhibition of Aubrey Beardsley's work at the Victoria and Albert Museum in 1966, and art deco, encouraged by the publication of such books as Bevis Hillier's *Art Deco of the Twenties and Thirties* in 1968, and films such as *Bonnie and Clyde* (1967). The aim was not to replicate past styles but incorporate them into a new, young look. Victorian furniture, reviled by serious connoisseurs of the decorative arts, was painted in bright gloss, and the new art of the poster was largely inspired by Aubrey Beardsley and Alphonse Mucha. Biba moved into the art deco former Derry and Tom's department store in the early 1970s, with retro, glamorous interiors by film-set designers.

'High Art' and mass culture now developed into one intermingled area. The pop art movement had begun in the early 1960s on both sides of the Atlantic with the work of artists such as Roy Lichtenstein and Andy Warhol in America and David Hockney and Allen Jones in Britain. The fine artists themselves took mass culture as their source of inspiration. Lichtenstein for instance reproduced the effect of the cheap printing of comic books in his paintings, which are made up of an overall pattern of dots.

Images taken from pop art were in turn used for posters, inexpensive crockery and murals. The exchanges operated on every level, as Warhol designed wallpaper with cows printed on it and furnished his studio, The Factory, in New York, with plastic silver clouds filled with helium. At the exhibition 'Four Environments by New Realists' held in 1964 at the Sidney Janis Gallery, New York, the pop sculptor Claes Oldenburg exhibited a bedroom setting that is an acknowledgement, if not a celebration, of consumer culture, with white vinyl satin sheets on the bed and a fake zebra-skin couch with a fake leopard-skin coat thrown over it. Oldenburg's soft sculptures of objects such as huge stuffed hamburgers were translated into furniture design, and cheap reproductions of his work were available at high street furniture shops for the youth market as late as 1988. The basement of the new Biba store by Witmore-Thomas featured gigantic mock baked-bean and soup tins on which were shelved real tins of food.

The op art movement was also to affect interior design. The movement originated in France with Victor Vasarely (1908–1997) and was developed in England by Bridget Riley (b. 1931), who painted black-and-white images designed to dazzle the spectator by giving the illusion of movement. Such images inspired television set-design for the programme *Top of the Pops* and boutiques, and generated a healthy poster trade.

Students at the Architectural Association in London had tired of the staid, permanent laws of the modern movement. 149 The Archigram Group, led by Peter Cook, released its first statement in 1961 expressing dissatisfaction with modernism and support for a more organic, free-flowing architecture. In later statements the Group declared an interest in the possibilities of an expendable architecture that could be adapted to suit the individual occupant. In Florence, the 150 Archizoom group, formed in 1966 and led by the architect-designer Andrea Branzi (b. 1938), made a similar foray into pop art aesthetics in 1967 with various beds that incorporated art deco motifs, images of pop stars and fake leopard-skin to indicate their allegiance to mass culture as opposed to the traditional high culture of architecture.

Pop design's challenge to notions about tradition and longevity was further emphasized by the production of disposable furniture. The lack of seriousness and playfulness of pop created an atmosphere in which furniture could be made from sturdy card, assembled by the purchaser, enjoyed

149 OPPOSITE ABOVE Archigram Group: design for an automated house.
150 OPPOSITE BELOW Archizoom Associates: 'Dream Bed', 1967. An Italian architectural partnership deliberately flout the canons of good taste with a mixture of art deco and pop motifs.

151 LEFT Chelsea
Drugstore, by
Garnett, Cloughley,
Blakemore Associates,
1969. A deliberately
disorientating interior
of aluminium capsules.
152 OPPOSITE Olivier
Mourgue: 'Djinn'
seating, as used
in the film *2001: A
Space Odyssey*, 1967.
Biomorphic forms
based on a steel frame,
foam padding and
jersey-nylon covering:
the 1960s flexible
furniture shapes.

for a month or so and then discarded as the next model
appeared. A paper chair by Peter Murdoch, in a simple bucket
shape and brightly decorated with polka dots, was mass
produced in 1964 for the British youth market and had an
expected life-span of three to six months.

Disregard for environmental issues was a characteristic of
pop. In the early to mid-1960s the consumer and designer were
wholly optimistic about scientific achievements. There was a
definite pro-technology dimension to the pop interior, which
exploited the possibilities of new materials and techniques.

151   The Chelsea Drugstore in King's Road by Garnett, Cloughley, Blakemore Associates (1969) used polished aluminium for its interior to create a spaceship atmosphere, enhanced by purple graphics in the style of a computer printout to indicate different areas within a large building.

152   In France, the interior designer Olivier Mourgue (b. 1939) created futuristic sets for the cult film *2001: A Space Odyssey,* furnished with his low, curved seating based on exaggerated amoeboid forms. The gently curved chaise longue 'Djinn' (1964) won him the AID International Design Award.

In Italy there was a marked reaction against mainstream modernism in the later 1960s, and young designers created interiors and furniture that deliberately challenged the canons of 'good taste'. The 'Sacco' seat designed by Gatti, Paolini and Teodoro for Zanotta in 1970 was simply a sack filled with polyurethane granules, adaptable and formless. Zanotta also manufactured early inflatable furniture with the 'Blow' chair by Lomazzi, D'Urbino and De Pas in 1967. Manufactured in clear PVC for use in swimming pools, its fun and anti-establishment

Consumer Culture

connotations appealed to young consumers in France and Britain. The same trio of designers was responsible for 'Joe Sofa', also manufactured by Zanotta in 1971 and consisting of a polyurethane-foam hand covered in soft leather in imitation of a glove. This fun furniture was inspired by the soft sculpture of Claes Oldenburg. The leading pop interior designer in Britain was Max Clendinning (b. 1924), who designed 'knock-down' furniture and total environments that relied on the use of one colour for their effect. His design for a living room, published by the *Daily Telegraph* in 1968, consisted of smooth, integrated solids for chairs, stools and tables, and storage space that was inspired by the excitement generated by space travel.

The appeal of new technology was accentuated with the first moon landing in 1969. Whole interiors were designed around

153–5 The informality of the 1960s living room exemplified by soft seating. Left, 'Joe Sofa', inspired by Claes Oldenburg's 'soft sculptures'. Below left, the 'Sacco' of 1970 and below right, the 'Blow' chair of 1967. Pop furniture mass-manufactured by Zanotta. Some shelves hung on painted walls or stacked on bricks, a bright-coloured moulded plastic table and a floor/table lamp were basics to be added.

156 Max Clendinning: dining room of the designer's own house, London, 1960s. Ceiling colours continue down the walls, horizontal stripes defy corners to expand space. Chair arms and backs are designed to be unbolted and exchanged for new shapes.

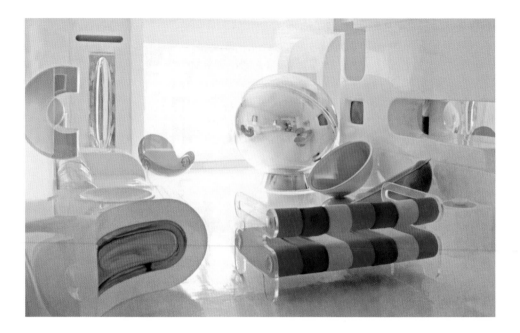

157 a space age theme, with computer typeface and metallic or brightly coloured plastic facings. The living room of Victor Lukens in New York (1970) incorporates all these features and includes an enclosed seating unit from which the occupant can observe the room without being seen.

The creation of deliberately disorientating interiors was a product of a new drug culture. Drugs that altered the perception, especially LSD, were associated with pop culture and gave rise to the Psychedelic movement. The normal dimensions of a room were obliterated by light shows, or by supergraphics which often imitated their effect.

In America Barbara Stauffacher Solomon popularized the use of large-scale graphics for the decoration of interiors
158 with the Sea Ranch Swim Club (1966) in Sonoma, California. Lettering was blown up and randomly mixed with bold stripes and geometric shapes in primary colours to conflict with the architectural space and produce a disorientating effect. In Britain, huge amoeboid shapes in bright, even fluorescent colours, spread randomly over ceilings, walls, doors and floors, as in the Junior Common Room at the Royal College of Art, designed by the students in 1968. There was also 'The Retreat Pod', designed by Martin Dean, which completely enclosed the occupant in an egg shape to encourage transcendental experiences. This type of interior had its ultimate expression

157 OPPOSITE Victor Lukens: living room, New York, 1970. The 1960s bubble chair, here in a oneway-mirror version, in the designer's own apartment of shiny moulded plastic and vinyl. Niches cut in the walls hold lights and television/sound equipment.
158 BELOW Barbara Stauffacher Solomon: 'Supergraphic', Sea Ranch Swim Club, Sonoma, California, 1966. The artist's bold red, blue stripes and graphics counterpoint the architectural space.

159 The 1960s conversation pit, suited to the relaxation of lifestyles and mores. Psychedelic neon (left), flexible tube lighting and giant stand-up electric light-bulbs were all popular 1960s–1970s designs.

in the sensory deprivation tank. The 'Trip Box' by Alex MacIntyre, a hallucinatory environment created with back-projection and music, was shown by the London furniture store Maples, in 1970, in an exhibition entitled 'Experiments in Living'.

Pop design inspired film sets, particularly those of *Barbarella* and *Help*, which introduced a carpeted seating-well. Effects such as these could be easily emulated at home and featured in previously staid magazines like *Vogue* and *House and Garden*.

There were strong links between pop and surrealism. The bizarre juxtaposition of incongruous objects in deliberate 'bad taste' in strangely lit, brightly coloured interiors stems from the language of Dada and surrealism. Previous proponents of surrealism like the critics Mario Amaya and George Melly were now deeply involved in pop. It is also an indication of the continuing importance of fine art for interior design, as the preferred alternative to architecture, which had anyway been discredited by movements like Archigram. The architectural elements melted away, as the room became an environment, a happening or a painting. The mural was a key feature of the pop interior. George and Patti Harrison commissioned the Dutch 'Fool' group of designers and artists to paint a psychedelic circular mural above the fireplace of their new bungalow in Esher, Surrey.

The brash, dayglo colours of the mid-1960s were tempered towards the close of the decade as concern about the environment became an issue. A new spiritual and political consciousness characterized youth culture, as a deliberately 'Alternative' set of rules was evolved. After the revolutions and student protests of 1968 and the *Torrey Canyon* oil-spillage disaster, young people were no longer pro-technology and sought ways to reject conventional Western values as hippies.

In terms of interior design, it was important to state your allegiances through the look of your home. Some abandoned permanent homes altogether for a nomadic lifestyle, preferring caravans or tent structures. In more permanent domiciles there was the introduction of artefacts from the Third World, particularly from India, natural materials, real fires, candle-light and patterned textiles and wallpapers. The *Whole Earth Catalog,* edited by Stewart Brand from 1968, provided such ecologically sound paraphernalia. One's room became a self-conscious political statement, whereas previously it had simply been fun. The book *Underground Interiors: Decorating for Alternate Life Styles* (1972) typifies this trend. The authors described it as 'an exploration into the revolt against old concepts of decor and old ways of living – a look at the new living environments closely linked to recent developments in art, politics and the press, all of which have taken the name "underground" to distinguish them from their establishment counterparts.' Whether 'radical chic', space age or surreal, these are anti-establishment interiors.

The return to nature was catered for by a new store called Habitat. Founded by Terence Conran, the first shop opened in

160

160 Habitat, London, 1972. By the early 1970s Terence Conran's store was marketing a quiet, tasteful but commercial modernism.

May 1964 in London to sell 'good' basic design to the middle-class market. The chicken brick, rush matting and beech furniture became standard in the early 1970s for the creation of a total lifestyle. The design of the shop itself was influential, with white-painted walls and a brown quarry-tiled floor. The goods were displayed *en masse* to give the impression of a warehouse. Significantly, Habitat also marketed classic modern movement chairs, signifying a shift in taste away from the exuberance of the 1960s. As the economic recession deepened young consumers rejected the freedom and transience of the 1960s.

One of the most lasting trends in late twentieth-century interior design was environmentally friendly or green design. This term emerged during the early 1970s, firstly in Germany, and signified an alternative and more caring approach to natural resources. The green movement was driven initially by minority political concerns and involved using consumer power. American designer Victor Papanek's (1923–1998) best-selling book, *Design for the Real World: Human Ecology and Social Change,* was first published in 1972 and acted as a critique of Western design practices, particularly built-in obsolescence, and advocated striving to meet consumer needs rather than wants. The book caused outrage among the design establishment.

It was not until the mid-1980s that green design and green politics shed their alternative image due to scientific research and legislation in support of an environmentally responsible approach. Green design became part of mainstream interior design practice and informed patterns of consumption. The recycling of household waste became the norm and consumers sought out environmentally friendly products. A public concern for green issues affected producers on a global scale. For example, the Valdez incident of March 1989, when a giant supertanker ran aground, spilling 10 million gallons of oil, which polluted 700 miles of coastline and devastated the wildlife, prompted the Valdez Principles. This set of guidelines was created by a multinational Coalition for Environmentally Responsible Economies (CERES), consisting of environmentalists and ethical investment organizations. The principles included protection of the biosphere, reduction and disposal of wastes, sustainable use of natural resources and energy conservation.

Green design has had an impact on the types of materials employed in interiors and on how space is used to create more environmentally friendly surroundings, making efficient use of natural light and sources of power. For example, a house designed by Javier Barba (b. 1949) in Llavaneres, at Maresme in Catalunya, Spain (1984–6), is partly buried in a hillside. It is well insulated by the turf, which covers the roof and blends into the garden; the main living area features a south-facing, curved window to exploit the available solar energy fully and tiled floors help to retain heat. The form of the interior is thus dictated by environmental concerns, particularly energy conservation. It is not only the careful management of finite sources that has made an impact on interior design, but also the need to create healthier working environments, particularly with the discovery of sick building syndrome in the 1980s. The need to ensure good systems of ventilation and natural sources of light, and to monitor the use of hazardous materials became central in the design of the workplace. The interiors of new office buildings, notably Niels Torp's (b. 1940)

161

161 Javier Barba: semi-buried house in Llavaneres, at Maresme in Catalunya, Spain, 1984–6. In the main living area the design of the interior is determined by energy-saving features, such as the curved, south-facing window and heat-retaining floor tiles.

162 Scandinavian Airways headquarters building near Stockholm, Sweden (1988), frequently feature a well-lit, central atrium. This enables occupants to enjoy the benefits of natural daylight, as offices either face outwards or overlook the central area, and of enhanced communication as workers circulate through the main walkway. The central atrium offers the opportunity to bring the external environment into the interior, another key feature of green design.

163 The atrium at the former corporate headquarters of PHICO (Pennsylvania Health Insurance Company) Group in Mechanicsburg, Pennsylvania (1976) features decorative greenery on the balconies, which overlook the central area. Likewise, in shopping malls such as Frank Gehry's (b. 1929)

164 Santa Monica Place in California (1979–81) or the one in Madrid illustrated overleaf, huge trees punctuate the internal space. In the domestic interior, a similar theme of nature working in harmony with the internal space of a building emerged as part

165 of green design. A weekend retreat (1999) designed by Takayuki Murakami and Mira A. Locher in Nasu, Japan, is arranged around a central courtyard, which features a mountain cherry tree. The rustic simplicity of the dwelling is enhanced by the walls, which have been treated with a rough mixture of ochre plaster mixed with straw and sand, contrasting with the

162 ABOVE LEFT Niels Torp: Scandinavian Airways headquarters near Stockholm, Sweden, 1988. The trend to provide a more conducive working environment has led to the widespread use of atria, such as this, for new office buildings.
163 ABOVE RIGHT Metcalf and Associates with Keyes Condon Florence: PHICO Group corporate headquarters, Mechanicsburg, Pennsylvania, 1976. The ambience created by this atrium is enhanced by the natural greenery that adorns the balconies.

cherry flooring and plywood veneer skirting boards. A house designed by British architect Bill Dunster (b. 1960) for himself features a triple-height conservatory on its south-facing facade that provides a space in which to grow plants and vegetables, and also an environmentally friendly living space, heated by solar energy.

The ethics of green design have also been applied by home-furnishing retailers to their goods. In 1989 Habitat ceased selling furniture made from tropical hardwoods because of

global concern about deforestation and instead their materials included rattan, which is derived from sustainable forests in Indonesia. In 1993 the Swedish home furnishing retailers IKEA bought Habitat; they are owned by the same founder, but operate as separate companies. Now a hugely popular mid-to-low-range global chain, IKEA has over 355 stores in twenty-nine countries worldwide, including India and Russia. With a similar commitment to green design, they only use environmentally friendly materials. For example, no cadmium is permitted in IKEA designs, as this heavy metal is both harmful and indestructible. They also sell organic cotton and linen furnishing products.

IKEA's mix of reasonably priced, high-styled design displayed in massive, out-of-town superstores, with carefully constructed room sets, is extremely successful. The adventurous designs are created by a Copenhagen-based consultancy, Pelikan, which acts as a design laboratory. Part of IKEA's success derives from the interactive relationship established with its consumers. The stores stimulate desire by offering a wide range of styles to suit different consumer identities and by promoting a do-it-yourself ethos. For example, in Britain, twelve types of fitted kitchen are offered in glossy modern or traditional wooden finishes at a reasonable price and customers are lauded in promotional material: 'One reason why even the solid-wood door fronts at IKEA are so astonishingly cheap is that customers assemble them at home... The job is ideal for a single weekend.' The personalizing of individual space by the consumer acting as their own designer was one of the most prominent trends in late twentieth-century interior design. It was capitalized upon by such stores as IKEA and also through books, magazines and television programmes, most notably *Changing Rooms.* Produced by the BBC, in this magazine programme two sets of neighbours, friends or relatives redecorated one room in each other's homes. An interior designer oversees the process, and part of the entertainment came from observing the tension between the amateurs and the professional. Considerable efforts were made to fit the interior to the inhabitants, to express individual tastes and identities.

167

167 IKEA 'Appläd' fitted kitchen, 2000. Stylish and simple to assemble, the Swedish furniture giant offer environmentally friendly goods for the active consumer.

Globalization in the 1990s inspired taste and the expression of identity in interior design. The speed of communication enabled by new technology, particularly the internet, and increased international travel raised popular awareness about design style and ethics. The Chinese art of feng shui – the organization of interior spaces around geomantic principles – is now immensely popular for both domestic and commercial interiors.

Design is a much more public concept today and consumers take a far more direct interest in the interior design process. Since the early 1970s interior design has existed as a specialization for the architect and as a profession in its own right: interior design can again be taken seriously and involve the consumer directly. And even if interior design is not permanent, it makes a statement of sorts about the inhabitant. The new self-consciousness in interior design has manifested itself in myriad styles and, since the early 1970s, made an important contribution to the creation of a post-modern aesthetic.

Chapter 8
The Post-modern Era

By the early 1970s the achievements of the modern movement had largely been discredited. In interior design as in architecture, a new pluralism was emerging. It was recognized that good design could no longer be measured by one mutually agreed yardstick. Interior design had come to the forefront of public design consciousness through its leadership of the retail revolution and the growth of interest in the domestic interior. A marked increase in the prosperity of certain social sectors, particularly of the young professional middle classes, led to a return to traditionalism and the revival of past styles in Britain and America. The bold experimentation of the 1960s was superseded by a period of retrenchment and revivalism.

Not all interior design of the 1970s was a reaction against modernism. The 'hi-tech' movement celebrated the aesthetic of industrial production, just as had Le Corbusier at the 1925 Paris Exposition, by introducing steel scaffolding, office furniture and factory flooring into the domestic interior. The work of architects has been crucial in the formulation of the style. Richard Rogers (b. 1933) in partnership with Renzo Piano designed one of the first hi-tech buildings, the Pompidou Centre, Paris, in 1977. Here all the apparatus for servicing the building is boldly displayed on the exterior of the cultural centre. The interior is less inventive, consisting of a shed with moveable walls. Rogers's design for the Lloyd's Building in London (1978–86) has the same flexibility as the Pompidou Centre, and is intended to be expanded in the future. The interior is centred around a twelve-storey-high, barrel-vaulted atrium that has been widely emulated in office buildings. Rogers successfully incorporates the old with the new by using the Lutine Bell as the focal point of the ground-floor area.

168

168 Richard Rogers: central atrium, Lloyd's Building, London, 1978–86. Essential services such as escalators are accentuated with colour.

169 Michael Hopkins: dining area of the architect's own house in Hampstead, London. Venetian blinds filter views and light between living areas.

169   In architect Michael Hopkins's own house, built in Hampstead, London, in 1975, the interior spaces of the steel-framed structure are delimited only by venetian blinds. *Hi-Tech: The Industrial Style and Source Book For The Home* (1978/9) by Joan Kron and Suzanne Slesin described how the domestic interior could now be assembled completely with mass-produced items ordered from trade catalogues. One of many interiors featured 170   in the book was the New York apartment of the designer Joseph Paul D'Urso, who had furnished it with a stainless-steel surgeon's sink, hospital doors, and metal fencing to subdivide the interior.

Although Le Corbusier used similar items in his Pavillon de l'Esprit Nouveau, there is a marked difference in aim between the two approaches. Le Corbusier was challenging the individualist, elitist world of the decorative arts by suggesting that well-made, functional but unfashionable mass-produced

170 Joseph Paul D'Urso:
steel-mesh fencing
for clothes storage
in the designer's own
apartment, New York,
mid-1970s.

objects should be used in the interior, whereas the aim of
hi-tech is to create surprising and chic interiors from obscure
sources. There is no element of social reform in this approach.
However, it could be regarded as an expression of changes in
attitude towards work and the home.

From the nineteenth century the two areas had been
distinctly separated, with the feminine sphere of the home
regarded as a temple of comfort and moral respectability, a
refuge from the workplace. With hi-tech the home becomes
like the workplace, with factory shelving in the kitchen, filing
cabinets and metal staircases and floors. In Victorian times
the bourgeoisie emulated their social superiors, proud to
display their leisured lifestyle. Work stopped at the front door.
In a period of unemployment the situation is reversed, and the

paraphernalia of work becomes a mark of status. For women pursuing a career, the hi-tech style suggests a functionally efficient home to be managed partly from the distance of the workplace.

The trend was mass marketed in the 1970s when Habitat launched its 'hi-tech' range of all-black minimal furniture. By the 1980s the style had become more refined, feeding into the vogue for upmarket minimalist interiors, and was joined by the recycling of industrial products. Ron Arad (b. 1951) salvaged seats from scrapped cars to convert into domestic seating which he sold at his shop, One-Off, in London. He has also used industrial materials in his designs for interiors, including 171 cast-concrete for the shop Bazaar, South Molton Street, London (1984–6), which marked a return to the New Brutalist use of deliberately rough, coarse materials for the interior. Huge broken slabs of concrete hung from rusty hawsers, and each clothing-rail was supported by a cast-concrete figure. This type of interior has been termed 'post-holocaust' because of its atmosphere of destruction and decay.

Other British designers to work within this industrial aesthetic in the 1980s include Ben Kelly (b. 1949) with his design for the Hacienda nightclub in Manchester (1984) and the headquarters of Pickwick Clothing (1989), and a group of designers brought together for an exhibition at the Crafts Council Gallery in London in 1987. 'The New Spirit' included furniture assembled from waste-wiring, bricks and rusty metal, to challenge accepted notions of comfort and taste by designers like André Dubreuil and Tom Dixon.

The 'hi-tech' movement also developed into a cool, super-minimal style during the 1980s. Rogers's contemporary, Norman Robert Foster (b. 1935), worked within the hi-tech aesthetic when designing the HSBC Building, Hong Kong, 173 and the interior of Katharine Hamnett's shop in Brompton Road, London (1986). Hamnett's shop, a nineteenth-century warehouse two storeys high, was left bare and almost empty apart from a few free-standing metal clothing rails and floor-to-ceiling mirrors on two sides to give an illusion of spatial infinity. As Adrian Dannatt observed in 1989, 'the late '80s has seen the development and consolidation of a revived, modified form of International Modernism as Interior Decoration, which manages the pressures of city life by ascetic exclusion rather than celebration. This purity in itself is in danger of becoming a cliché, a "timeless" look that will be easily classified ever after as 1980s Timeless style.' Interior designers such as the Czech-born Eva Jiřičná (b. 1939), in her sparse designs for Joe's 174 Cafe in London (1986) and the Joseph Shops, incorporated

171 Ron Arad: clothes shop Bazaar, London, 1984. Concrete was cast on site for the figures (of workers on the project) and the curtain, using imprints made by means of a vacuum and granule-filled plastic cushions. The figures doubled as window display and rail supports.

172 Ron Arad: recycled seat of a Rover car, 1982, the first such piece to be marketed, and the start of a 'recycled furniture' movement in Britain.

173 Norman Foster Associates: Katharine Hamnett's shop, South Kensington, London, 1986. A glass bridge, underlit, passed through a tunnel to emerge into the vast, pure-white space, with mirror-walls to reflect the customer.

175

industrial materials like aluminium, matt-black cladding and tensioned-steel cables to produce a mood of control and understatement that has now been widely emulated. The New York studio that Vignelli Associates designed for themselves also emphasizes simplicity, with interest provided by unusual materials like the lead which covers the walls and corrugated, galvanized-metal screen which divides the service area from the design studio. The work of David Davies for the retail chain Next incorporated light woods, pale colours and mirrors to create a spacious, 'tasteful', uncluttered shopping environment, and revolutionized the appearance of retail outlets, building societies and banks. The minimalist style which still owes a debt to modernism is in total contrast with the fussiness of the major movement of the period: post-modernism.

174 ABOVE Eva Jiřičná, Jiřičná Kerr Associates: Joseph flagship store, London, 1980s.

175 LEFT Vignelli Associates: the architects' own studios, New York City, 1985. The interest lies in the use of unusual materials such as waxed lead and galvanized steel. Formal inspiration comes from the sculpture of Donald Judd and Richard Serra. Moulded-plastic and steel furniture was specially developed for the project, and manufactured by Knoll.

176 OPPOSITE Michael Graves: sitting area, Crown American Building, Johnstown, Pennsylvania, 1989. Graves uses revival Josef Hoffmann armchairs with his own designs for cabinet, tables and carpet.

Like hi-tech, post-modernism was rooted in architectural practice. The American architect Robert Venturi (1925–2018), whose first book, *Complexity and Contradiction in Architecture* (1966), was an early polemic on the subject, expressed a growing dissatisfaction with the narrowness of the modern movement and argued that historic styles and the visual immediacy of mass culture had something to teach the architect. This was further elaborated in *Learning From Las Vegas* (1972). Venturi offered visual arguments with the 'Architectural Chairs', which are all alike in profile but refer to different styles when seen from the front. There is a brightly coloured example of an art deco chair, complete with sunrise motif, and a 'Sheraton' chair with swags and other stylized classical details. The architect-designer Michael Graves (1934–2015) also contributed to the post-modern debate in America with his Public Services Building, Portland, Oregon (1982), and furniture for the Italian-based Memphis Group.

The architectural theorist Charles Jencks was responsible for bringing post-modernism into a wider cultural context in his book *The Language of Post-Modern Architecture* (1977). He used the structural analysis of language, which had been developed

in Switzerland by Saussure and later in France by linguists such as Althusser, to analyse and create his own designs. He designed houses in Britain and America, including the interior of his own 'Thematic House' in Holland Park, London, in which he clustered reception room and bedrooms around an enclosed spiral staircase. Jencks self-consciously manipulated the symbolism of past architectural styles in his furniture designs, marketed by Aram Designs as 'Symbolic Furniture'. In the various rooms he has drawn upon past styles as diverse as the Egyptian and gothic to represent the different seasons. In the library the furniture is based on Biedermeier models, while the tops of the bookcases refer to different architectural styles.

177

Italian design played a prominent role in the creation of post-modern interior design. By the late 1960s small groups of avant-garde designers had grown frustrated with the slickness of the Italian design image. In 1972 the influential exhibition 'Italy: The New Domestic Landscape', held at the Museum of Modern Art, New York, showed specially commissioned micro-environments by the leading radical designers Ettore Sottsass (1917–2007), Mario Bellini (b. 1935) and Joe Colombo (1930–1971) that challenged accepted ideas about the home environment and about modernism. Bellini's 'Kar-a-Sutra' consisted of a large bright-green car with transparent roof and sides. Sottsass and Colombo, inspired by space travel, designed modules for various functions which could be rearranged, allowing the inhabitant more flexibility. In 1979 the Studio Alchymia was formed in Milan by Alessandro Mendini, who had succeeded Gio Ponti as the Editor of *Domus*. Sottsass joined the group, but in 1981 formed his own Memphis Group of designers.

178

179

180

From the time of their first public exhibition at the Milan Furniture Fair in the same year, the Group had an enormous impact on interior design. They flouted the notions of good taste that had become so closely bound up with modernism in Italy, and designed within a post-modern aesthetic. Furniture was faced with brightly patterned plastic laminate. Inspiration came from mass culture. Design was intended to be part of the mass-consumer experience. Sottsass's furniture designs were witty, bold, and intended to be fun. The 'Carlton' room divider, designed by Sottsass for the Milan Fair of 1981, is covered

181

177 OPPOSITE Charles Jencks: library, Thematic House, London, 1979–84. Symbolic elements include post-modern bookcases (for books on post-modern architecture), and the frame of the interior window that resembles a face and is also layered to allude to the wall's construction. The honey-and-black of the furniture echoes the Biedermeier chair, but in the case of the slide-container tower (left) is painted onto a steel cabinet.

178 LEFT Mario Bellini: 'Kar-a-Sutra', a hybrid car-seating unit, shown at the exhibition 'Italy: The New Domestic Landscape', New York, 1972.

179 BELOW Joe Colombo: 'Total Furnishing Unit', shown at the 1972 exhibition. The block comprises four units to cater for all basic human needs: kitchen, bathroom, cupboard, and 'bed-and-privacy' unit (left) fitted with a step-in cabin for seclusion and pull-out day-and-night furniture.

180 ABOVE Memphis Group and Abraxas: sitting room, Singapore, 1986. The furniture includes 'Astoria' chairs by Matteo Thun, 'Atlas' table (centre) by Aldo Cibic, and lights by James Evanson and Martine Bedin. The colours of the specially woven carpet and column were chosen to tie all the pieces together. The paintings are by graphic artists working for Sottsass Associates.
181 RIGHT Ettore Sottsass: 'Carlton' room divider, 1981.

The Post-modern Era

with brightly coloured plastic laminate that imitates marble, and takes on unconventional shapes which challenge accepted notions of storage. Pieces are often out-of-scale and use forms seemingly inappropriate to furniture, for example a seating unit by Umeda based on a boxing ring, one of which was bought by fashion designer Karl Lagerfeld for his house in Monte Carlo. The French decorator Andrée Putman (1925–2013) advised Lagerfeld on buying furniture from the first two Memphis collections. His high-rise apartment, decorated in 1985, had grey-painted walls in order to allow the furniture to dominate.

The Memphis style had instant appeal, and although it originated as furniture design, was widely influential

182 LEFT Andrée Putman: office commissioned by Jack Lang, Minister of Culture, Paris, 1985. Smooth golden-blonde furniture contrasts with gilt panelling.
183 OPPOSITE Ronald Cécil Sportes: sitting room, private apartments for President Mitterrand, Elysée Palace, Paris, 1983. Note Sportes' wire mesh chair (centre).

on interior design in America, Japan, and throughout Europe. The surface patterns of George Sowden (b. 1942), an English member of the group, were widely emulated in, for example, the interiors of mainstream shops and fast food outlets during the 1980s. Post-modernism in Italy denoted challenging design based on the images of 1950s mass culture.

In France there has been a Renaissance in interior design since the 1960s. As well as her work for Karl Lagerfeld, Andrée 182 Putman's commissions include the office of the Minister of Culture in Paris (1985). In this prestigious setting the classic French *boiserie* (wall-panelling), chandelier and window treatment are deliberately and dramatically contrasted with drum-shaped post-modern chair, semi-circular desk and hi-tech lamp. French official encouragement of post-modern design contributed to the vivacity and success of French interior design in the 1980s. The President of the Republic, Mitterrand, commissioned several leading young designers to decorate the private apartments of the Elysée Palace in 1983, among them Jean-Michel Wilmotte (b. 1948), Philippe Starck (b. 1949) 183 and Ronald Cécil Sportes (b. 1943). Again, in this traditional palace, post-modern decoration inspired by, for example, Viennese design of the 1900s, art deco and hi-tech is used to create a striking mix of the antique and the contemporary.

French interior designers have also enjoyed success in Japan. Marie-Christine Dorner (b. 1960) worked with Wilmotte from 1984. In 1985 she designed a range of sixteen pieces of post-modern furniture for the Japanese Idée furniture company, two boutiques for Komatsu and a cafe in Tokyo.

In Britain designers like Dinah Casson (b. 1946) used the motifs of post-modern design successfully. For example, the Gran Gelato shop in King's Road, London (1984), shared the wit, combination of disparate motifs and strong colours of Italian post-modernism. The architect Terry Farrell (b. 1938) designed the TV-AM building in the post-modern aesthetic, and was particularly careful to design a complementary interior and furniture.

A striking effect of post-modernism in America and Britain has been to open the floodgates for traditional design. The message of Venturi, Jencks and Memphis was to broaden design beyond the limits of the modern movement. Under its impetus, architects like Quinlan Terry (b. 1937) and Robert Adam in Britain have been able to create whole Georgian-style buildings for offices and homes. For architects like these, modernism was a brief and unfortunate interlude in the everlasting narrative of classical architecture.

The return to traditional values has generated a whole movement back to the revivalist interior on both sides of the Atlantic. The rules of classical architecture that inspired Edith Wharton and the work of traditional decorators like the American Mrs Henry Parish II have never been more popular. Nineteenth-century decorative painting techniques like marbling, ragging and stencilling became a vogue. For those unable to afford the luxury of an interior decorator, a whole market has evolved in educational courses, books, television programmes and magazines for the amateur. Jocasta Innes introduced the subject of decorative paint finishes to a wider public with her book, *Paint Magic* (1981). Retailers specializing in ready-to-wear clothing such as Marks & Spencer entered the market for home furnishings, and like Innes brought the English country house look, first popularized by Colefax & Fowler, to a wider market. The appearance of the home has become a major preoccupation, partly as a result of a property boom and partly as a result of more women working outside the home. More money is available for home furnishings as the standard of living rises, and many women regard spending on the home as a top priority.

The interior design heritage also influenced designers in a more imaginative way. Nigel Coates (b. 1949) has taken the example of nineteenth-century eclecticism to create interiors

184 Terry Farrell: reception area, TV-AM, London, 1983. Exaggerated classical details are contrasted with witty post-modern chairs.

that celebrate the splendid decay of Europe. As the leader of a group of Architectural Association students known as NATO (Narrative Architecture Today), in 1983 he exhibited an eccentric collection of found objects and free-form drawings that suggested structures for architecture rather than delineating them in a clear-cut plan and model. His flat in London (1981) was an essay in architectural metaphor, juxtaposing different period styles and artful decay like a self-conscious and deliberate stage set.

185 Nigel Coates with Shi Yu Chen: interior of Caffè Bongo, Tokyo, 1986. Termed by the designers the 'theatrical image cafe', the interior incorporates narrative signs from Pompeii, Rome, the Italian 1950s and modern Tokyo. The aircraft-wing balcony with raked columns supports classical-style statuary. Paintings and objects by a number of European artists and designers include a pendant light by André Dubreuil.

Illustrations of the flat were shown in the Japanese magazine *Brutus,* and as a result he was commissioned to design the Metropole restaurant in Tokyo in 1986. Here classical columns, swags and *trompe l'œil* painting evoke the atmosphere of the London gentlemen's club brought completely out of context and exaggerated. Similarly the work of Powell-Tuck, Connor and Orefelt relies on the inspiration of expressive drawings and the perverse use of historical motifs. The entrance hall of pop entrepreneur Marco Pirroni's London flat of 1985 by David Connor is almost a piece of three-dimensional art in itself, in the spirit of the expressionist film sets of *The Cabinet of Dr Caligari.* As part of a reaction against mainstream modernism, some interior designers, whether architecturally trained or not, have moved towards fine art and literature as their sources of inspiration. The deconstruction movement, whose early manifestations include the 'Deconstructivist Architecture' exhibition at the Museum of Modern Art in 1988, and the deconstructivist seminar at the Tate Gallery, London, in the same year, was based on the literary theory of the French writer Jacques Derrida. The applications of the theory to interior design involve the taking apart of the elements that make up the interior. The work of the American SITE Projects, Inc. could be considered within this context. Their design for a door (1983) had an area of laminate stripped layer by layer to make a through hole. Their architectural work for Best Products Company, Inc. during the 1970s resulted in buildings which appeared to be disintegrating, with gaps in the wall and piles of bricks incorporated into the design. More recent Deconstructivist architect-designers include the American Frank Gehry with his Winton Guest House, Minnesota, and Behnisch and Partners of Germany with their Hysolar Institute Building, University of Stuttgart. The interior of this small building on the edge of the university campus is tremendously exciting and energetic. As in the Schröder House (p. 70), there is a central axis from which the interior spaces almost explode. The staircase linking the two floors and a connecting ramp meet in a chaotic angular mix of window frames, roofing, steel supports and cladding. The architects have deliberately composed an interior that looks as if it may fall apart, a loose collection of different technological and structural elements.

As Japan has established herself as a world leader in terms of trade, so she has become more confident in the language of traditional design. Just after the war national architecture had connotations of reaction and the right wing, and the new building programme was dominated by the American brand of mainstream modernism. Now the Japanese have

186

186 Behnisch and Partners: stair head and ramp, Hysolar Institute, University of Stuttgart, 1987.

187 rediscovered their rich architectural heritage, and interiors like those of Fumihiko Maki (b. 1928), Kisho Kurokawa (1934–2007) and Takefumi Aida (b. 1937) have the clarity and asymmetry of traditional Japanese design. Other Japanese architects responded to the late-1980s romantic eclecticism of figures such as Coates, which led to something of a stylistic free-for-all.

This plurality of style continued throughout the 1990s. The accent was placed on process rather than form. Green design is one example of this trend, with designers under a legal as well as a moral imperative to take environmental concerns into account. Paradoxically, with the rapid developments in technology, the need to incorporate new materials and communication systems into the commercial and domestic interior also became prevalent. The design of office space

187 Kisho Kurokawa: restaurant for Hiroshima City Museum of Contemporary Art, 1988.

in the 1990s was hugely affected by the use of electronic communication. The trend was to 'hot desk', whereby no individual worker has their own permanent desk, but uses one of a series of bookable spaces. For example, the British Telecom (BT) Westside building at Hemel Hempstead (1996), designed by architects Aukett Associates with the interiors by Interior PLC, was the workplace of 1,250 sales, marketing and customer centre personnel. Flexible working practices were supported by the provision of open-plan workstations for team members to share, plus 'touch down' desks for more casual use. There were also meeting, conference and video rooms. Work today is often carried out beyond the office, at home, in transit, with customers, or in hotels. New technology enabled the BT workers to communicate via portable computers and mobile phones, accessing the internet. The interior design of an office space such as Westside encourages informal interaction with strategically placed coffee areas and atria.

The rigid office spaces of the earlier part of the twentieth century, which represented and reinforced tight, bureaucratic

188 Aukett Associates/Interior PLC: British Telecom Westside building, Hemel Hempstead, UK, 1996. The impact of technology means that office interiors are now more flexible, with multi-purpose spaces shared by a mobile workforce.

189 Capella, Larrea and Castellvi: dancefloor at Pacha Leisure Centre, near Tarragona, Spain, 1992. Technology, in the form of video, lasers and fibre-optic lights, enhances the dancefloor experience.

structures, have been superseded by a more flexible layout to enable informal teamwork. The interior design of the meeting room must also change to take new technology into account, but whatever the actual style of the meeting room, the plasma screen, installed for the display of electronic information, must be designed so it can be concealed when not in use. The possibilities of new technology were not only exploited in the office, as leisure centres such as the Pacha Leisure Centre near Tarragona, Spain (1992), by Juli Capella (b. 1960), Quim Larrea (b. 1957) and Jaume Castellvi show. This huge nightclub covers an area of 5,677 square metres (61,000 square feet). The main dancefloor is illuminated and also transparent, suspended over a swimming pool. Lasers, video-walls and shimmering fibre-optic lights add to the headiness of this late twentieth-century dance space.

189

The domestic interior has also been affected by new technology. By the late 1950s the television replaced the open fire as the focal point of the main living space. However, now that television screens are flat and can be placed on any wall,

the possibilities for room layouts have opened up. Stylistic heterogeneity continued to be the prevalent trend in the late twentieth century, with an inexhaustible range of styles available to reflect individual identities. Individual identities can also be reinforced or explored through the recent phenomenon of boutique hotels. Originating in New York, these interiors are themed to reflect different tastes. It is the function and use of domestic and commercial spaces that have changed, due to the impact of new technology, and look set to change in the future.

190

190 André Balazs and Christian Liaigre: Mercer Hotel, New York, opened 1997. An elegant warehouse conversion, this boutique hotel offers the New York experience of loft-conversion living.

Chapter 9
The Sustainability of Interior Design

What are the dominant themes in interior design in the early decades of the twenty-first century, the age of post-industrial globalization? In general, the boundaries between architecture, fashion, graphics, fine art and the interior have become less rigid. Architects have become more interested in interior design, and artists have explored the built environment as part of their creative practice, in works such as *House* (1993) by Rachel Whiteread (b. 1963), a cast of the interior of a Victorian terraced house. There is also less emphasis on style in the twenty-first century compared with the twentieth: commercial interiors are dictated more by corporate identity and branding than by high style. And the subject of interior design has recently become the focus of a more sustained level of academic enquiry. But the overriding issue is that of sustainability, which has grown in importance on a global level, and for the field of design generally. As awareness about issues such as scarce resources and global warming is raised, so government policy in the developed world calls for a more responsible use of precious materials and energy. This has led to a change of emphasis from fashionability to building usage and careful use of resources.

Today, interior designers are acutely aware of the need to use woods from renewable sources – materials regarded as exotic in the art deco era, such as ebony, are now banned in an attempt to halt deforestation in tropical and temperate rain forests. Other materials, such as bamboo, a highly renewable source, are recommended for flooring, wall decoration and furniture construction. Bamboo does not need replanting and grows organically, without the need for fertilizers or pesticides. The toxicity of materials is also of concern, and interior designers are increasingly aware of the properties of certain plastics or

191 Kelly and Masoko Neville: a self-build house created for the Channel 4 series *Grand Designs* in 2007. The central focus of this sustainable interior is an 800-year-old oak tree from which the wooden staircase was fashioned. The house is hexagonal and was inspired by Tolkien's *The Hobbit*.

synthetic paints. The lifecycle of materials must also be borne in mind, and acceptable levels of disposability or recycling attained. Bamboo is again ideal, as it can be composted, rather than buried in landfill sites. Indeed, designers are now expected to conceive not only the style and appearance of an interior, but also its integration into the eco-system.

There has been a marked increase in self-build projects using sustainable materials: approximately nine thousand such homes are built every year in the United Kingdom alone.

191 The Eco House in Cambridgeshire, for example, which featured on Channel 4's *Grand Designs* television programme, is an oak-framed house, with straw insulation. The central staircase was carved from a single, 800-year-old oak tree, salvaged by the owner-builder. The house has large windows and a lantern in the roof, which enhances the flood of natural light into the house and saves on power. The power itself is supplied by a wind turbine. Sustainability extends to public buildings too.

192-4 One extreme example, the Icehotel in Jukkasjärvi, Sweden, runs an annual competition in which entrants are invited to design ice interiors for its lobby and bedrooms. Carved from ice in organic forms, the entire building melts in the spring to be rebuilt afresh in winter.

A sustainable approach to materials is enhanced by the careful use of energy. Interior designers can, for example, make better use of natural light and exploit the latest technology in glazing design, choosing photochromatic, thermochromatic or electrochromatic glass for windows. This new generation of 'smart' glass can reduce the amount of glare entering a building from the sun: in the case of photochromatic glass, the windows automatically darken when exposed to solar rays, thus saving on air-conditioning costs. Thermochromatic glass fulfils the same function, but darkens when the glass reaches a certain temperature. Electrochromatic glass can be altered by means of an electric current – on the Ferrari Superamerica sports car, for example. The Revocromico window in the car's roof can be darkened by the driver using a switch; it happens automatically when the car is parked to prevent fading of the interior and overheating.

Thresholds between the exterior and interior have become less distinct as buildings are opened up to the outside world and natural light is used as a feature of the design. Ventilation can also be introduced, rather than wasteful air conditioning,

195 as with the so-called Gherkin Building in the City of London. Designed by Foster and Partners for the financial company Swiss Re, in the heart of the business district, the building's structure means that it uses fifty per cent of the energy normally employed for a building of its height. A series of atria spirals within the steel framework, acting like lungs for the distribution of air in the forty-one storeys and 76,400 square metres (822,000 square feet) of floor space. The space-rocket profile was dictated by the confines of the site, and the external pressure differentials help to drive the air circulation within. The club

192–4 Icehotel, Jukkasjärvi, Sweden, 2006. The hotel is designed and built every year by carving out interiors in the ice. A competition is held annually for the design of the interiors. Opposite above, Doug Meerdink and David E. Scott: 'The Helices', ice suite 310. Opposite below, Mikael Nille Nilsson, Mark Armstrong and Åke Larsson: 'Absolute Icebar'. Above, AnnaSofia Määg: 'Bubbleboil Swamp', ice suite 301.

The Sustainability of Interior Design

195 TOP Foster and Partners: Swiss Re Building, London, 2004. Nicknamed the Gherkin because of its pickle shape, it is arguably the first environmentally sustainable office skyscraper. On the 40th floor, at the very top, is a bar that offers a panoramic view of the city through the vast expanses of glass and skeletal structure.

196 ABOVE Zaha Hadid: interior, BMW plant, Leipzig, 2004. The production line for the 3-Series cars circulates at ceiling height through the staff canteen and reception area, past the terraced open-plan offices.

room at the very apex of the building offers spectacular views across the city, enhanced by extensive glazing. The BMW plant (2004) built by Zaha Hadid (1950–2016) in Leipzig, Germany, used a similarly fluid approach to inside and outside and allowed the flexibility to accommodate different functions within the building. The central building is the nerve centre for the mass production of BMW's 3-Series cars, and pulls together the separate functions of the production areas – body-shell unit, paint shop and assembly area. The most striking aspect is the part-assembled cars that move along a track around the building through areas such as the staff canteen and the reception area.

The Eden Project in Cornwall, England, reflects the growing public interest in ecological and environmental issues. Opened in 2001, three huge geodesic domes, structures shaped like part of a sphere, house plants from different global climates to raise awareness of our dependency on the natural world.

197 Nicholas Grimshaw: interior of the Eden Project dome, Cornwall, 2001. A geodesic dome provides a micro-environment for tropical plants.

198 Diller Scofidio+Renfro: interior of the Brasserie, Seagram Building, New York, 2000. A classically modernist interior has been refurbished to preserve the authentic experience of dining at the Four Seasons restaurant, with twenty-first-century touches.

The architect Nicholas Grimshaw (b. 1939) used a twin-layer steel structure for the domes and ethylene tetrafluoroethylene (ETFE) film, an extremely hardwearing plastic, for the panels, to enhance the solar energy within by allowing maximum light penetration. In 2006, The Core was added as an education space, constructed in an organic, spiral structure made from wood.

Alongside new builds with sustainable elements, there is also a trend to refit and refurbish existing buildings: a sign of increased interest in sustainability and in the historic past. For example, the Brasserie restaurant in the archetypal modernist Seagram Building in New York was refurbished in 2000. Originally designed by Philip Johnson in 1959 as the Four Seasons restaurant, it was damaged by fire in 1995. Seagram were anxious to preserve the fashionable appeal of the restaurant, and employed Diller Scofidio + Renfro to redesign the space. They kept the modernist style by using sage-green vinyl to cover the tall booth dividers. A vast wave of dark timber envelopes the main dining area, which is spectacularly lit to enhance the drama of entering the restaurant by means of the glass, steel and stone staircase. A video installation, which plays sequentially on a series of fifteen monitors above the bar, is based on Diller and Scofidio's Para-site installation at the Museum of Modern Art in New York (1989) and shows film of visitors entering the building.

The Seagram scheme preserved and enhanced the original use of a space: a significant proportion of architectural design work is about remodelling buildings and reshaping them to signify one type of use rather than another. Instead of the resource-intensive design and construction of brand new buildings, with the attendant problems of waste disposal, disused buildings, usually industrial, are being given a new lease of life. For example, Matchworks in Liverpool, developed by Urban Splash from 2001, is a group of office spaces created from the former Bryant and May match factory. Other key examples can be found in the field of museum design. Tate Modern in London, originally designed by Sir Giles Gilbert Scott (1880–1960) in 1939 as a power station, is now London's prime space for the display of modern and contemporary art. Rather than disguise and attempt to supplant the building's original purpose, the Swiss architects Herzog & de Meuron

199

199 Urban Splash: office interior, Matchworks, Liverpool, 2004. The vast industrial space, built between 1919 and 1921 for the mass production of matches, was taken over by Bryant and May in 1923 and eventually closed in 1994. The factory has been remodelled to create rentable office space.

exploited the might of the vast Turbine Hall as the key public space of the building. Industrial materials are laid bare. Five storeys high and 152 metres (500 feet) in length, it is the key circulatory focal point of the interior. The shop, cafe, stairs and lifts are all visible from this space, and the three gallery floors overlook it. Headline-grabbing shows, including *Test Site* (2006) by Carsten Höller (b. 1961), which brought funfair slides to the art gallery, and Ai Weiwei's (b. 1957) installation *Sunflower Seeds* (2010–11), have been situated in the hall. At the top of the building, Herzog & de Meuron added two glazed storeys, with a restaurant and bar, affording views of the River Thames and the footbridge engineered by Ove Arup & Partners and designed by sculptor Anthony Caro (1924–2013) and architect Norman Foster (b. 1935), which takes pedestrians to the financial district of London and to St Paul's Cathedral. Such an opening up of a pre-existing building to the outside world, making less of a distinction between the exterior and the interior, is a common element in many such remodelling projects.

The Great Court in London's British Museum was reconfigured by Foster and Partners in 2000. The existing building opened in 1852, and was designed in the fashionable Greek Revival style by Sir Robert Smirke (1780–1867). The original domed, circular Reading Room, designed by Smirke's brother Sydney (1798–1877), was added to the empty quadrangle at the heart of the building between 1854 and 1857. With piecemeal additions throughout the nineteenth and twentieth centuries, the British Museum was in need of a complete revamp and a higher profile for its commercial enterprises and education space, owing to the massive increase in visitors, now numbering five and a half million a year. Foster preserved the newly restored Reading Room at the centre of the two-acre space and used a bespoke computer system to design the glazed roof, which consists of 3,312 individually shaped triangular panes, supported in a steel framework. It adds light and a sense of space, which the original design lacked, and opens up the previously enclosed courtyard to more natural daylight and the outside world.

Foster and Partners added a similar structure to the

Reichstag, the German parliament in Berlin, in 1999. Following the collapse of the Berlin Wall, and with it communism, in 1989, the Reichstag, originally built in the nineteenth century as a

200 OPPOSITE Herzog & de Meuron: Turbine Hall, Tate Modern, London, 2000. This vast industrial space acts as an awe-inspiring setting for contemporary fine art. The old power station's machinery was removed and a steel structural framework installed within the brick shell of the old building to create seven new floors.

201 Foster and Partners: Great Court, British Museum, London, 2000. A specially engineered roof opens up the central space to light. The new space gives a focus to the museum for circulation of visitors, retail and education.

symbol of the newly united Germany, was radically reworked. The building had been burnt out by anti-Nazi agitators in 1933, the ensuing outrage in part strengthening Hitler's new position as chancellor. It was further damaged during the Second World War. Attempts at using the interior were made during the 1960s, but by then the importance of the building had diminished, as the national government of West Germany now met in Bonn. Mezzanine floors were added and other internal additions were made between 1958 and 1972, which Foster subsequently removed. With Germany reunited again in 1990, Berlin became the capital once more and a focal point for new corporate buildings, including the spectacular Sony Centre by Helmut Jahn (b. 1940), which consists of eight buildings, grouped around a glazed atrium, employed as residences, shops, offices and entertainment centres. The new Reichstag uses glazing in a similarly adventurous way, with a spectacular dome rising out of the centre of the nineteenth-century shell. Visitors may enter the dome and view the parliament below through a glass floor.

202 Foster and Partners: interior, Reichstag Dome, Berlin, 1999. The new dome allows visitors to enjoy a panoramic view of the reunited city and to observe the parliament at work through the glass panel in the centre.

Panoramic views of the city can be enjoyed from the spiralling ramp within the dome. The entire interior of the Reichstag was removed and replaced with modern materials and open spaces, but the focus is the glazed dome, which diminishes the barriers between government and the public.

203 Hotel design has also seen the imaginative recycling of existing buildings. In Holland, the Kruisherenhotel in Maastricht, designed by Henk Vos (b. 1939) in 2005, reworked the interior of a fifteenth-century monastery and gothic church. Part of the Camille Oostwegel Château Hotels & Restaurants chain, the hotel has an entrance in the form of a copper-lined, trumpet-shaped tunnel. The reflective qualities of the material are capitalized upon with fluorescent lights embedded in the concrete floor. This leads to the reception area, once the nave, which now has high-end designer furniture and lighting, and a glass elevator. A new mezzanine floor was created directly above the reception area to house the restaurant, providing views through the vast gothic windows of the streets of Maastricht beyond. A conference room leading off the restaurant is housed in an electrochromatic glass cube, which can be made either clear or opaque white at the flick of a switch. The guest rooms, situated in the former monks' cells, have been simply decorated, with digitally enlarged copies of paintings and photographs and modern furniture. Gothic details are juxtaposed with sleek contemporary furniture in

203 Henk Vos: interior of the Kruisherenhotel, Maastricht, 2005. A gothic church has been remodelled as a hotel, with the restaurant on a newly constructed mezzanine to the right. The copper-lined entrance tunnel can be seen on the lower left.

204 Jestico & Whiles: interior, Malmaison Oxford (formerly Oxford Castle), 2006. The top floor of the former prison has been reworked as a boutique hotel with cells transformed into luxury rooms.

the public areas to create surprising effects. This trend is seen elsewhere within the hotel industry. For example, Malmaison Oxford, an old prison, has luscious interiors designed by Jestico & Whiles; the erstwhile cells have become the guest rooms. Malmaison, a British hotel chain, has pioneered the innovative reuse of buildings for their chic city-centre hotels. In Belfast, a nineteenth-century dockside warehouse has been utilized, incorporating bare brick and industrial ironwork alongside unconventional contemporary furniture. The small lift is padded in deep purple velvet. The juxtaposing of the luxurious with the industrial (or, in the case of Oxford, with a prison) is the chain's highly successful trademark.

A slightly different approach to hotel design has been taken by fashion designers, who are now much more likely to explore the boundaries between clothing design, retailing and bespoke interior design. For example, the French fashion designer Christian Lacroix (b. 1951) remodelled a seventeenth-century bakery in Paris into a couture hotel with the help of architects Cabinet Vincent Bastie. The small, exclusive Hotel

205 Christian Lacroix: interior of the Hotel du Petit Moulin, Paris, 2004. In the reception, 1960s Swedish design mingles with decorative luxury in the Marais district.

du Petit Moulin opened in 2004, with only seventeen rooms, each resembling a stage set decorated with sumptuous Lacroix signature fabrics and gold trimmings. Pop furniture from the 1960s is blended with classic modern and Zen to create a cacophony of distinctive colour and style. Other fashion houses who have seized the opportunity to enter the hotel world include Armani, with the Armani Hotel Dubai, Bulgari in Milan and Bali, Palazzo Versace on the Australian Gold Coast, Cerruti in Vienna, Düsseldorf, Dubai and Brussels, and Ferragamo in and around Florence.

The establishment of fashion brands through flagship store design has also increased. Prada, for instance, reconfigured the former SoHo branch of the Solomon R. Guggenheim Museum in New York, originally a nineteenth-century warehouse, with an interior by Rem Koolhaas (b. 1944) of the Office for Metropolitan Architecture (OMA) in 2001. OMA are best known for uniting the latest technology with cutting-edge architectural theory. The entrance and ground floor are comparatively empty, dominated by a round glass lift, with the main store in the basement. Another key feature is the sweeping blond

206

206 Rem Koolhaas, Office for Metropolitan Architecture (OMA): interior of Prada store, New York, 2001. A zebrawood wave structure connects the two floors, with steps to the right and cages containing clothing displayed above.

zebrawood structure that connects the two floors. Clothing is suspended in cages from the ceiling, and the transparent changing-room walls turn opaque white when the rooms are in use. The Prada store, or Epicenter (2003), in Tokyo, designed by Herzog & de Meuron, is another example. A glazed structure

207

207 Herzog & de Meuron: interior, Prada store (Epicenter), Tokyo, 2003. The futuristic interior features only a database for the stock, with a minimal quantity of clothing on display.

surrounded by a landscaped area, unusual for Tokyo, provides a hallmark stylish and simple building. Digital projections and databases of the collections are found in the store. Haute-couture shops such as this find resonance in the capital cities of the developed world, as the motivation is to offer luxury goods at high prices to maintain exclusivity and the brand's status.

208 Branding also dominates other market sectors where values and attractiveness are communicated through interior design. For example, sports giant Reebok opened its new world headquarters just outside Boston, Massachusetts, in 2002, establishing an entire 'Brandscape'. Designed by NBBJ architects, the four edifices are linked by Reebok's unmistakable sportswear brand image. The walkway leading into the building is in the form of a running track, and the interior is sleek and streamlined, with the different elements flowing effortlessly into one another. Reebok's identity is reinforced in all aspects of the company's designs, from trainers to high-street stores and the look of their headquarters. Brand recognition is therefore assured.

209 The sportswear company Nike has opened a series of Nike Towns in major cities throughout the world, including New

208 NBBJ: interior, Reebok headquarters, Canton, Massachusetts, 2002. The new corporate headquarters is entered via a road modelled on a running track, which leads to this integrated, flowing space.

York, Berlin and London, with vast and minimal interiors. At the London flagship store the stock is sparsely in evidence: the space is devoted to reinforcing the brand through blown-up images of sporting heroes, a vast projector screen showing sporting events, and a floor decorated with layouts of games courts. Loud music pumps throughout the stores, creating an

ambience that accentuates youth, sport and energy. Such an emphasis on a consistent corporate identity produces interiors that are seemingly designed irrespective of where the space is located geographically. Criticized by some writers, particularly Naomi Klein in *No Logo* (2000), as a form of North American hegemony, this consistency does ensure the global appeal, or at least the recognition, of the brand. Retail spaces are now carefully designed to attract particular sections of society: in the case of Nike Town, the target is the younger consumer interested in the fashion appeal of sportswear and physical fitness. A similar approach was taken in the interior design of the 4-you Youth Savings Bank in Krems, Austria, created by the Unit in 2000. In contradiction to the conventional interiors of banks, which emphasize solidity and respectability, the 4-you Youth Savings Bank was designed to appeal to the younger generation. The floor is bright blue with the yellow markings of a baseball court. A huge baseball-glove seat, based on the Zanotta 'Joe Sofa' (1971), invites lounging, and the informality is reinforced through a row of PCs rather than cash desks.

Mandarina Duck, an Italian luggage firm, creates wacky, off-the-wall objects for a sophisticated adult consumer. Droog Design was selected to design their prestigious Parisian store

209 OPPOSITE Nike in-house
design team: interior, Nike
Town, 5th Avenue, New York,
1997. Global brand identity is
reinforced with the emphasis
on youth and athleticism.
210 RIGHT Nike in-house
design team: London flagship
store, Oxford Circus, London.
This vast retail space is
sparsely decorated to allow
the projection of sporting
imagery on a giant scale.
211 BELOW Unit (Wolfgang
Bürgler and Georg Petrovic):
interior, 4-you Youth Savings
Bank, Krems, Austria, 2000.
A baseball theme is used to
attract and reassure teenage
savers.

using their playful corporate image. Founded by Renny Ramakers (b. 1948) and Gijs Bakker (b. 1942), Droog Design made their mark with their first show at the Milan Furniture Fair in 1993, when they challenged preconceptions about users, objects and space. Issues of sustainability are a key element in their work. Rag Chair by Tejo Remy (b. 1960), for example, is a collection of discarded and disused materials and clothing, tied together with belts to form a chair. Remy has also reused discarded milk bottles, hung from rods in the ceiling in sets of twelve to create lamps. Mandarina Duck purchased a property on Paris's prime designer shopping street for their flagship store. The two-storey space was remodelled with plain white ceilings, walls and floors with free-standing objects, or 'cocoons', used to display the merchandise. The cocoons were labelled 'circle', 'tunnel', 'wall', 'curtain' and 'enclosure'. The 'wall' consists of one wall with metal pins, used to clasp the luggage for sale, and another is made up of red, yellow and green rubber bands stretched horizontally, into which the bags are inserted. The shoppers are guided through the store by means of a curtain made of thin, curving translucent plastic strips. A three-and-a-half-metre, doughnut-shaped metal container conceals clothing, and customers are encouraged to discover the merchandise through encounters with unfamiliar objects. More like an art installation than a shop interior, the concept had to be easily translatable for Mandarina Duck's international chain of stores.

An ambience of conviviality and relaxation has been created through the interior design of the global chains of coffee shops. Starbucks, the first and most famous, was established

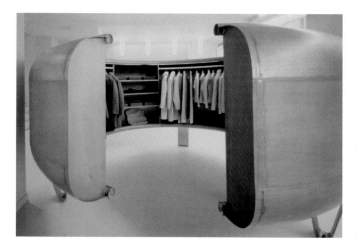

212 Droog Design: interior, Mandarina Duck, Paris, 2001. An example of the 'cocoon' constructed in the boutique interior to display clothing, concealed inside the structure.

213 Virgin in-house design team: interior, Virgin Atlantic aeroplane, upper-class suite, 2006. Competition for prime passengers is played out through the provision of luxury and comfort on boring long-haul flights. Chairs convert into beds and optimum personal space is ensured through screens.

in Seattle in the 1970s, embarking on its worldwide expansion in 1987. The owner, Howard Schultz, used the expertise of other global brands such as McDonalds, Pepsi and Kentucky Fried Chicken in his bid to expand, and by 2018 Starbucks had stores in seventy-six countries. The phenomenal success of Starbucks can be partly explained by its reinforcement of core corporate values through the nature of its stores. Jazz plays gently in the background and newspapers are available, as customers relax on leather sofas, surrounded by tasteful artwork and the aroma of coffee. Urbane and sophisticated, the dark wood surroundings enhance the gourmet image of real coffee.

Global branding also dictates the interior design of transport. For example, the Virgin brand is used to sell products and services as diverse as cable TV, mobile phones and wedding planning. Originally founded as a record retailer in 1970 and then a record label, the company built an image of youthfulness and entrepreneurship. In 1984, it launched Virgin Atlantic Airways in direct competition to the more established (and the more establishment) British Airways. Its familiar red-and-white logo is displayed everywhere, from the tailfins right through to the marketing materials. As competition to gain passengers for airlines becomes more vigorous, so Virgin Atlantic attracts more exclusive clients using 'design', by offering unique beds in the upper-class suite, for example. The interior design of aeroplanes goes beyond the usual questions of style, materials and use; issues of space and safety have also to be considered, as well as the added dimension of weight. The problem of fitting beds into a restricted space was solved by Virgin Atlantic's in-house design team in an ingenious way. The beds convert

213

The Sustainability of Interior Design

214 Claudio Lazzarini and Carl Pickering: enclosed deck of the *118 WallyPower*, 2004. The designers have eschewed traditional nautical styling for this technically innovative, luxury yacht. A glass-sided deckhouse shelters a capacious but sparsely furnished saloon with white upholstery, plain wooden flooring and surrounds. The steps down to the cabins are centrally placed, followed by the modernist dining area and controls beyond.

from seats, which are upholstered in leather; with the touch of a button the chair flips over and the other side is covered in supportive foam. The upper-class suite also features a bar area.

The interior design of boats is a similarly specialist field with more limited parameters than land-based interior design. Before the advent of mass air travel in the late 1950s, ocean liners were the most common means of international travel. The interiors of the ships very often reflected the national identity of the line owners, as on the British-owned Cunard Line and the French-owned French Line. In the post-war era, the designs were undertaken by star architects and designers. James Gardner (1907–1995), Dennis Lennon and Hugh Casson (1910–1999) designed for Cunard's flagship *Queen Elizabeth 2* (1969) and Gio Ponti for the Italian *Giulio Cesare* (1951). Ship interior design is now mainly concentrated on the cruise market, where waterborne holidays are provided en masse in floating, glitzy hotels that cater for an older clientele, dominated by the North American market. The *Queen Mary 2,* which entered service in 2004 for the Cunard Line, features a six-storey central atrium, casinos and multifarious entertainment spaces designed by Tilberg Design, based in Sweden. There has also been a growth in yacht design for the luxury market. Wally, based in Monte Carlo, was founded by the Italian Luca Bassani (b. 1956). In 2004, the firm commissioned architects Claudio Lazzarini and Carl Pickering to collaborate on the interior design of the *118 WallyPower.* The design team makes no reference to traditional nautical styling, and instead has placed a geometrically shaped glass structure on top of the wooden deck. The space within is completely open plan, with a dining table for sixteen and a flight deck rather than a cockpit; reaching speeds of up to 63 knots, the boat is powered by gas turbines.

214

If there is one style that distinguishes interior design in the early twenty-first century, it is the 'non-style' of minimalism. The minimal style has had an impact on the domestic interior, as the impetus from the media is to declutter your home, use neutral shades and negate individualist style. This makes a home easier to sell, but has meant a move away from a cosy, family home. The chief exponent of the minimal style is British architect John Pawson (b. 1949). His stripped-back interiors are void of what he regards as unnecessary ornament and clutter. Pawson designed a series of minimalist shops for Calvin Klein: the first, a new building, opened in Tokyo in 1994, and in 1995 the New York store opened. An existing neoclassical building on the corner of Madison Avenue, with plain white walls, pale stone flooring and precision lighting, was reworked. He repeated the formula with the Calvin Klein store in Paris, which opened in 2002, again using pristine minimalism to reflect the sparse and simple identity of the American fashion brand. Pawson's style was also used to maximum effect in the design of the Nový Dvůr Monastery in the Czech Republic. The original Baroque manor house lies at the heart of the monastery, designed as a home for forty Cistercian monks with new sleeping cubicles and a church. It is perhaps appropriate, given that his designs for domestic spaces resemble monasteries, that Pawson has now turned his hand to designing a real one.

215

A more emotionally sustainable and spiritual dimension is detectable today in some aspects of interior design practice, as designers struggle with the global impact of their work and critically evaluate design's broader contribution to culture and society. This is evident in the psychological use of colour and light in public buildings such as prisons and hospitals. There is also a growing tendency among interior designers to develop

215 John Pawson: interior of Chapel, Nový Dvůr Monastery, Czech Republic, 2004.
The minimalist style is ideal to create a spiritual space for prayer and reflection.

as reflective practitioners, taking theoretical issues into account as part of their practice. The study of the interior is now more academically respectable. Where once it was seen as lacking the gravitas of product design or graphics, it has begun to emerge from the dominance of architecture as a discipline in its own right. Since 2000 there has been a marked increase in publications about the history and theory of the subject. Edited collections such as Susie McKellar and Penny Sparke's *Interior Design and Identity* (2004) and Hilde Heynen and Gülsüm Baydar's *Negotiating Domesticity: Spatial Productions of Gender in Modern Architecture* (2005), and theoretical analyses such as Charles Rice's *The Emergence of the Interior: Architecture, Modernity, Domesticity* (2007), have added significantly to the field of study. *Intimus: Interior Design Theory Reader* (2006), edited by Mark Taylor and Julieanna Preston, presents the key texts for the development of the subject. Monographs of individual designers and decorators have also been published, including Penny Sparke's *Elsie de Wolfe: The Birth of Modern Interior Decoration* (2005). Practising architects, who previously had not considered interior design as central to their practice, now write on the subject: for instance, New York-based architect Joel Sanders's essay 'Curtain Wars: architects, decorators and the twentieth-century domestic interior' (2002) describes the professional architect's longing to be involved in interior decor. These publications, along with the founding of the Modern Interiors Research Centre at Kingston University, London, mean that the academic subject of interior design has now been firmly established.

The latest developing trend in interior design is that of the interactive interior. In the domestic space, lighting can be fitted that reacts to the occupants' movements within a room, or even their mood. Developments in new technology also make the complete convergence of all home entertainment possible, creating the intelligent living space. Electronic companies such as Panasonic are working on technology for the future, with a home cinema and television system that can be projected onto a white wall. An entire wall could be decorated with projected images, which the inhabitant could specify and arrange as they wished, with built-in alarms and message possibilities. Entry to the home need no longer be by key, but can be controlled by retinal scanner. The possibilities of new technology are set to challenge the interior designer and consumer alike, within both public and private spaces. Interior design has been turned virtually inside out: as the Victorian home analysed at the beginning of this book was designed to keep the threat of modernity at bay, so now the results of technology determine the appearance and use of interior space.

Chapter 10
Transnational Interiors

The emergence of new technologies and the resulting ease and speed of communications and travel around the planet have opened up a new era of transnational interior design. The worldwide web, cloud storage services and software programs for interior design such as Vectorworks make international working far easier than ever before. Whether in, between or across Africa, the Americas, Asia, Australasia or Europe, many of the styles and visual arrangements of the interior share the same language as designers are now able to transcend national boundaries. Modernism continues to be the all-pervasive style, whether for luxury apartments, airports or shopping centres across the globe. But Europe can no longer claim exclusive rights to modernity. It is important to recognize that interior design in this post-colonial context often combines the traditions of the local culture and ambitions for the future, layered with the latest aspects of modernity. Different and complex histories are played out in the interior that connect with one another across regions, nations and continents. This complex balance between the perceived authenticity of tradition and the currency of global modernism for a neo-liberal economy is characteristic of contemporary interior design around the world.

Emerging from the dominance of colonial or imperial power and revising histories of colonial and imperial rule, human spaces of interaction are an important place for these shifting relationships to be played out. The use of the term transnational opens up the coverage of this chapter beyond the conventional Western focus, which places America and Europe at the centre, as does most of this book. Shifting power relations, patterns of immigration and the circulation of design ideas signal a new era for interior design beyond Western norms.

To begin with, newly liberated countries selected modernism as the unifying style of choice to express their new, international aspirations. For example, India was liberated from British rule in 1947. In a commission led by Prime Minister Jawaharlal Nehru, Le Corbusier was selected to design a complete new capital city of Chandigarh for the Punjab region, as the previous capital, Lahore, was now located in Pakistan following Partition. At first Le Corbusier declined the offer, but then the British architects Jane Drew (1911–1996) and Maxwell Fry (1899–1987) persuaded the modern architect to take on the commission along with his cousin, Pierre Jeanneret. Le Corbusier visited the country intermittently but Fry, Drew and Jeanneret lived there for three years while the project took shape during the 1950s. Le Corbusier designed the master plan and the Capitol Complex while the rest of the team, with the help of several Indian architects – M.N. Sharma, A.R. Prabhawalkar, B. P. Mathur, Piloo Moody, U.E. Chowdhury, N.S. Lamba, Jeef Lal Malhotra, J.S. Dethe and Aditya Prakash – concentrated on the civic, domestic, educational and retail aspects. The new city was created for a population of 500,000 housed in fourteen standardized dwelling types with two or three storeys, constructed mainly of brick as this was more economical. Even the most basic of the dwelling units had a kitchen, electricity, running water and sanitation. Jane Drew in particular attempted to work with the future inhabitants of the scheme and talked to them about their requirements. As a result she added pre-cast screens or *jalis* and ensured there was sufficient cross-ventilation within the interior space. The majority of the scheme was an example of tropical modernism, with the International Style transposed from Europe to Asia with minimal adjustment to local traditions and cultures. However, this was the aim of Nehru, who was attempting to unite a divided state with universal modernism as his chosen vehicle.

A similar approach was taken in Singapore. This tiny city-state in Southeast Asia gained independence from British rule in 1959 when it became part of the free-standing Malay Federation. In 1965 Singapore became independent of the Federation under the leadership of Prime Minister Lee Kuan Yew and a modernist building project was instigated under the state-controlled Housing & Development Board (HDB), under which entire towns were built featuring high-rise blocks in modernist style. The interiors of these urban flats were also modern, and the state promoted this style by means of the free magazine *Our Home* from 1972 until 1989. Distributed to every HDB home on a bi-monthly basis, the publication advised on simple, modern design and good taste, including the avoidance of clutter. This programme of social engineering was hugely successful and the universal style of modernism united the diverse population of Chinese, Malays and Indians. The percentage of the local population living in public housing was increased from 9 per cent in 1959 to 23 per cent in 1965, and from 1985 at least 80 per cent of Singaporeans lived in HDB flats. The interiors of the flats are predominantly white and simple in layout. The inhabitants were able to make changes within their homes with, for example, the Islamic Malay residents including a prayer room while some Chinese inhabitants realigned their interiors according to the rules of *feng shui* and built in altars.

While the examples of Chandigarh and Singapore used modernism as a unifying force that negated local, diverse traditions, the work of the Sri Lankan architects Minette de

216 ABOVE Pierre Jeanneret: Type 4j house, Chandigarh, India, 1950s.
217 OPPOSITE Living room of a Housing & Development Board flat in the 1980s. Published in *Our Home* magazine, Housing & Development Board, Singapore.

Silva (1918–1998) and Geoffrey Bawa (1919–2003) are key examples of indigenous, post-colonial design. Ceylon was under British rule from the nineteenth century until Sri Lanka was created in 1948 from the former British colony. De Silva and Bawa are best known as leading practitioners of critical regionalism, and designed within local idioms combined with Western modernism as a critique of tropical modernism, the style of architecture practised by Le Corbusier, Pierre Jeanneret, Jane Drew and Maxwell Fry in India as well as West Africa during the 1950s and 1960s. Minnette de Silva was the first Asian woman to be elected to the Royal Institute of British Architects (RIBA) in 1948, having initially trained in India and then at the Architectural Association in London. She returned to her native Sri Lanka in 1948 to contribute to the building of this new nation, setting up her practice in the family home in the city of Kandy.

De Silva then designed a series of private dwellings that translated the modernist style to the needs and traditions of this tropical island. The Dr P.H. Amarasinghe House in

218

218 ABOVE Minnette de Silva: View across the open plan towards the entrance.
Dr P.H. Amarasinghe House, 1960. Colombo, Sri Lanka.
219 OPPOSITE Interior of dining room with Tulip chairs, 33rd Lane, Colombo,
Sri Lanka. Geoffrey Bawa Trust.

Colombo of 1960 was open plan with columns for support,
allowing for a fluid use of space with the use of portable screens.
The outside and the inside space flow into one another and lush
vegetation fills the interior as well as the exterior. Another key
feature of de Silva's work is the incorporation of the internal, open
courtyard or Kandyan *mada midula*, where the outside became
part of the inside with no roof. De Silva also encouraged local crafts
and used traditional cane and open-weave divans and lounging
chairs, stools, mats, cushions and small carpets. These were
always distributed sparingly within the interior and could be
moved around easily due to their lightweight construction. This
reflected the lifestyle of the Sri Lankan residents, with extended
family occasions and Buddhist festivals easily accommodated
within the flexible space. De Silva employed the young Danish
architect Ulrik Plesner during 1958. However, Plesner grew tired of
the provincial life of Kandy and the financial insecurity of working
with de Silva and left to work with Geoffrey Bawa in Colombo.

Bawa's designs for hotels, universities, government buildings and homes throughout Asia and particularly in Sri Lanka are renowned as sympathetic to their surroundings and culture, but mindful of modernist precepts. Less well known is the evolving interior design of his own home, 11 33rd Lane in Colombo, during post-colonial times. The interior of Bawa's own home from 1960 until 1998 is a fascinating tableau of the combinations of colonial and post-colonial influences. Bawa's home interior is poignant, as its development during these years mirrors the subtleties of post-colonial experiences for the designer. The building is now preserved as a museum by the Bawa Trust. It includes antique furniture from the Dutch period of occupation as well as the British. These heavy Victorian chests and chairs are directly contrasted with examples of mid-century modern furniture including Eero Saarinen's Tulip chair, which was

made in replica on the island due to import restrictions during the 1960s. Nineteenth-century Ceylonese antiques also find a place in the interior, as do contemporary Sri Lankan craft objects and art. This carefully curated interior also features modern Finnish glass by Olva Toikka, perhaps reflecting the transnational influence of Ulrik Plesner.

The case of Sri Lanka demonstrates how interior design can be used for the containment and working through of colonial pasts in a post-colonial present, without obliterating local heritage and conditions. A similar example was developed in Ahmedabad, the former Gujarati capital in India, by Le Corbusier for Mrs Manorama Sarabhai, a member of a prosperous textile family. The Sarabhais were instrumental in the newly independent India led by Nehru from 1947 in promoting Indian design through the creation of the Calico Museum of Textiles in Ahmedabad in 1949 and the founding of a design school there in 1961. The National Institute of Industrial Design, now the National Institute of Design, was the first organization devoted to teaching design at tertiary level in India. Manorama Sarabhai's house was built from 1951 to 1955. The open-plan house with large picture windows was built from brick and concrete with a garden on the roof. The owner furnished her new home with a mixture of Western furnishings and a rich array of Indian handcrafts. There were traditional hand-printed cottons from Rajasthan and Le Corbusier designed divans in the form of traditional Indian *charpoy* beds made from rosewood and wicker. Indian metalwork was also used to decorate the home with cast-bronze occasional tables, vases and candlesticks from South India.

220

In direct contrast, more recent domestic spaces in India pay less attention to precedent or a personal, bricolage approach and adopt a contemporary, transnational approach. For example, the World One skyscraper apartments in the Indian financial capital of Mumbai (2017) are built on the former site of textile factories. The three apartment blocks are typical of a new type of gated community that has become popular with the burgeoning Indian middle classes and upper middle classes based there. The building consists of three towers. Two are 52 floors high and one is 117 floors, the highest structure in the city. Designed by the American architects Pei Cobb Freed & Partners, the exterior of the buildings is one of bland modernism twinned with the impact of height.

221-2

Access to the interiors is restricted and sophisticated technology is used to police the thresholds, including three-dimensional X-ray vehicle scanners at the entrance, face-recognition and fingerprint technology for entering the

220 Le Corbusier: Sarabhai House, Ahmedabad, India, 1951.

lifts and biometric locks on the individual apartments. As a reflection of colonial residences there is a separate entrance for service staff, who no longer live on the same premises as their employer, as in the days of the Raj, but attend on a daily basis. This is an exclusive property and an exclusive address, made separate from the world beyond the security fence where residents can enjoy their own medical facilities and business centre, with no need to venture beyond the 17-acre, bounded island site. There are stunning views from the balconies and refreshment areas: the outside world is visible but kept at a safe distance.

The interiors were designed by the Italian-based Armani/ Casa and roll out the designer's familiar stylistic range. The luxury interior design company was established in 2000 by the leading minimalist fashion designer Giorgio Armani (b. 1934). Armani/Casa was launched with a flagship store in the design capital of Milan and featured furniture inspired by the art deco designer Jean-Michel Frank. Art deco glamour continues to be an inspiration for Armani, and is combined with high-end materials to create simple yet luxurious

surroundings in a limited palette of taupe, grey and beige. There is fretwork, exquisite craftsmanship and detailing in the World One interiors, with the metallic reflections of white gold leaf, liquid metal and special wall finishes, which pay subtle homage to the rich iconographic culture of the host country.

African design is prospering with a sustained effort to reappraise the significance of the past for the future of the fifty-three disparate and varied nations that make up this huge continent. It is being put into the service of healing the scars of a troubled past with a type of design that draws on local tradition with a futuristic element. The importance of contemporary design for Africa is evident with the establishment of the first Museum of African Design (MOAD) in 2013 in the Maboneng Precinct in downtown Johannesburg. This cavernous former industrial building was refitted to showcase contemporary African design work. Although the museum closed in 2017, the will to support contemporary design in Africa remains. Cape Town was the World Design Capital in 2014 and in 2017 the African Architecture Awards 223 were inaugurated. The overall winner was the uMkhumbane Museum in Durban, South Africa, by South African designers Choromanski Architects, founded and led by Rodney Choromanski (1961–2018). This local community resource was commissioned by the eThekwini Municipality to preserve the complex cultural and political history of the Cato Manor region and the city of Durban. The area was densely populated in the 1920s and 1930s as black Africans settled there and rented land from Indian market gardeners because apartheid meant they could not settle in the city of Durban. However, during the 1950s and 1960s there was one of the biggest forced removals in South African history, and the museum acts as a focus for the retelling of these shared narratives through events and exhibitions. It also acts as a location for the preservation of Zulu history. Three materials were used for the construction of the museum: a laser-cut aluminium shell with pierced shapes to echo Zulu symbols, red brick laid by local craft workers, and a concrete frame. The striking atrium is illuminated by the shapes formed by the aluminium exterior.

The ceremony for the African Architecture Awards took place 224 in the Zeitz Museum of Contemporary Art Africa (MOCAA) in Cape Town. Hewn out of an imposing concrete grain silo, this

---

221 OPPOSITE ABOVE Armani/Casa Interior Design Studio: World One, Mumbai, 2019. Interior featuring fretwork.
222 OPPOSITE BELOW Armani/Casa Interior Design Studio: World One, Mumbai, 2019. Interior featuring textiles (the master bedroom).

223 Choromanski Architects: uMkhumbane Museum, Cato Manor, Durban, 2017. Client: eThekwini Municipality.

224 Thomas Heatherwick: atrium, Zeitz Museum of Contemporary Art Africa (MOCAA), Cape Town, 2017.

remodelling was led by British designer Thomas Heatherwick (b. 1970) and provides the first large venue for contemporary African art. Opened in 2017, the interior of the existing building, which consisted of a multitude of cement tubes, was cut in an asymmetrical form to create a stunning atrium lit from above. Two glass lifts travel the height of the building in the original concrete tubes, which have been reinforced with a new casing. The exhibition spaces are conventional white cubes, dropped into the concrete structure. Controversially, the top floors of the building are a luxury hotel that Heatherwick did not design and are rather gaudy in contrast to the measured greyness and whiteness of the museum.

High-profile examples of architecture such as these help to propel Africa onto the global stage. But the majority of Africa's city governments have scarce resources and the cities show signs of physical neglect and decay. A sizeable majority of the population live in basic accommodation, often remodelled with recycled materials. The Ghanaian-British architect David Adjaye (b. 1966) undertook an extensive photographic survey of African metropoles for the series of books *African Metropolitan*

Architecture (2011), but all his photographs are of street scenes and portray a continent of great beauty and colourful decay with no views of interiors. Interior design is at a nascent stage, with few interior design university degree courses – there are only three in Southern Africa, in Botswana, Lesotho and South Africa, with interior architecture being offered at the University of Pretoria. The only post-graduate course is run within South Africa, the country that tends to be the dominant force in African design. The interior design profession has recently established its own professional organization, the South African Institute of the Interior Design Professions (IID). This provides a forum for interior design professionals in South Africa but was only established in 2006 and is perhaps still dominated by architecture, frequently regarded as the more important discipline when it comes to something as significant as forging a post-colonial identity.

The United Arab Emirates (UAE) has seen a massive building programme over the past thirty years as the different states that make up the alliance aim to become global cities, attractive to tourists and multinational companies. Dubai is one of the seven Trucial States and was governed by a British protectorate from the nineteenth century, with Britain controlling both defence and international relations. This governance was withdrawn in 1968 and Dubai played an important role in the establishment of the new alliance, no longer dominated by Britain, in the form of the UAE. Dubai looked to its traditions and its history to reinvent itself as an important tourist destination and trading centre. 'Personalized Hospitality Amidst Arabian Splendour' is the tagline for the luxury hotel Burj Al Arab (Tower of the Arabs), which has become the icon of Dubai. Situated on an artificial island, the building is in the form of a traditional sail of an Arabian *dhow* or sailing ship and was designed by the London-based multinational engineering and design firm WS Atkins. Led by architect Tom Wright, the building was completed in 1999 with 202 luxury duplexes over 28 double storeys.

225-6

The luxury interiors were designed by Chinese-born Khuan Chew (b. 1953), the founder and principal designer of KCA International, which now has offices in London, Dubai and Hong Kong. She studied at the London College of Furniture and worked for the British interior designer David Hicks and eminent American hotel interior designers Dale and Patricia Keller. Chew worked closely with Dubai's ruler, Sheikh Mohammed bin Rashid Al Maktoum, to signal aspects of Arabian history and culture combined with luxurious baroque, Empire and art deco touches. The sumptuous Talise Spa

225 KCA International: atrium of Burj Al Arab, Dubai, UAE.

Transnational Interiors

226 KCA International: Talise Spa pool, Burj Al Arab, Dubai, UAE.

on the eighteenth floor uses as its colour scheme the four colours of the UAE flag, green, red, black and white. The hotel features luxurious materials including gold, rich mosaics and fabrics, which makes it one of the world's most popular high-end destinations.

The vast majority of interiors included in this book are enclosed, comfortable spaces, hermetically sealed from the outside world. Whether the interiors are backdrops for stylistic tropes or vehicles for the expression of individuality, a global brand or post-colonial identity, proximity to the outside world is not a priority. However, one important trend in twenty-first-century interior design is that of inside out: the interior spaces of private and public buildings are becoming more and more linked to the spaces of the exterior. The Victorian padded parlour was a place of reclusion, of hibernation from the threatening world of modernity with one single, standard door leading to the rear garden. In direct contrast, many interiors of recent years positively open up to the world outside, to the natural world beyond the bricks and mortar or concrete and plastered walls of the inside, perhaps with a balcony city view – as in the case of World One – or of fish swimming in the ocean, as in the restaurant of Burj Al Arab. The popularity of the bi-folding door, for example, has made the threshold between the interior space and the space to the rear of the home invisible. The doors, made from wood, metal or UPVC, and fully double-glazed, run along a track and can be opened and folded away against the wall completely, opening up the interior space to the outside. This space-augmenting device is particularly popular with city dwellers eager to open up their homes and add more room to their property. The market has grown by 12 per cent annually since 2008 and manufacturers supply new builds as well as residents undertaking home improvements. The same floor covering can be used inside and out to negate the division further. This has been made possible by new technology, including secure thermal glass and fittings. But this permeability is only a feature of the private rear of the interior and never occurs on the street.

Bi-folding doors and even folding doors demonstrate a technological virtuosity whereby the way objects are arranged in space seems effortless, but relies on sophisticated systems and materials. These key technological changes, additions, integrations and interventions have become more pervasive and have altered the human interface with the interior. Not only can we make a wall disappear to view the outside, we can also experience a different reality within the interior space. Technology has greatly affected the perception of the world around us, requiring us to face reality instantaneously on the one hand, and yet giving us permission to slip into timeless, immersive fantasies on the other. The divisions between outside and inside have become more porous, with virtual worlds and lived experiences colliding and coalescing.

227 The Alchemist boutique of 2011 by Miami-based Rene Gonzalez Architects displays technical virtuosity in the amazing installation of a rectangular, 160 square metre (1,726 square foot) glass box into the fifth floor of a concrete parking garage designed by the Swiss architects Herzog & de Meuron. The equivalent of thirteen car parking spaces in size, the shop appears to be suspended between the concrete slabs, with extensive views of the Miami skyline from this unlikely base. The boutique sells a range of outré labels from its cutting-edge premises. A series of holes in the floor provide a flexible location for the display stands and a range of kinetic mirrors reflect the street below or the skyline above. This dynamic sense of motion within the space is enhanced by sensors that move forty-three pneumatic, mirrored ceiling panels in concert with the shoppers, coming to a halt when they do and moving when they do. The system was designed by London-based

Random International, an art and technology company that specializes in the creation of unusual spaces using the latest technology. Its most famous installation is *Rain Room* (2012), which mimics the visual and aural sensation of being caught in a rainstorm without the visitor getting wet as the complex technology senses human presence. The artwork is now in the collection of Los Angeles County Museum of Art as well as the Sharjah Art Foundation in the UAE. Random International is a transnational project, with staff hailing from Africa, Asia and Europe, and the aim is to explore the post-digital world within a fine art and interior design context.

In the post-digital world and age of automation it is possible to answer your front door remotely and talk to your caller by video, even if you are on the other side of the world, with gadgets such as the Nest video doorbell. Using smart technology it is possible for robotic devices to vacuum the floor and devices such as the Amazon Echo wireless speaker can be told via voice commands to send and receive emails, make calls, play music, dim the lights in any room or even tell jokes. This is a boon particularly for the housebound, including the disabled and the elderly. In addition, virtual reality devices are becoming more sophisticated and can now take us anywhere in the world for a truly transnational experience or science fiction future.

227 Rene Gonzalez Architects: Alchemist boutique, Miami, 2011.

Select Bibliography

General

Bachelard, Gaston, *The Poetics of Space*, Boston, Massachusetts, 1969. A lyrical exploration of spaces in the home, from rooms to drawers.

Brooker, Graeme, and Lois Weinthal (eds), *The Handbook of Interior Architecture and Design*, London, 2011.

Calloway, Stephen, *Twentieth Century Interior Decoration*, London, 1988. Good source particularly for the more expensive, exclusive type of interior.

Clark, Clifford Edward, *The American Family Home, 1800–1960*, University of North Carolina Press, 1986. Contains useful information on the ordinary dwelling.

Coulson, Anthony J., *A Bibliography of Design in Britain, 1851–1970*, London, 1979. Lists further sources for research.

Csikszentmihalyi, Mihaly, and Eugene Rochberg-Halton, *The Meaning of Things: Domestic Symbols and the Self*, Cambridge, New York, reprinted 1999. An excellent introduction to the ways in which interiors reveal clues to their occupants from an anthropological viewpoint.

Deschamps, Madeleine, 'Domestic Elegance: The French at Home' in *L'Art de Vivre, Decorative Arts and Design in France 1789–1989*, London, 1989. General outline of French developments.

Forty, Adrian, *Objects of Desire: Design and Society 1750–1980*, London, 1986. Stimulating account of the relationship between mass-produced design and society.

Friedman, Joe, *Inside London: Discovering London's Period Interiors*, Oxford, 1988. Excellent illustrations and valuable information on surviving interiors which may be visited.

Fuss, Diana, *The Sense of an Interior: Four Writers and the Rooms that Shaped Them*, London, New York, 2004. Investigation of interiority and how it affected the lives and homes of four writers.

Heskett, John, *Industrial Design*, London, 1984. Particularly useful for German design.

Hitchcock, Henry-Russell, *Architecture: Nineteenth and Twentieth Centuries*, London, 4th edn, 1977.

McKellar, Susie, and Penny Sparke (eds), *Interior Design and Identity*, Manchester, New York, 2004. A collection of essays that looks at the interior in relation to gender and social class.

Myzelev, Alla, and John Potvin (eds), *Fashion, Interior Design and the Contours of Modern Identity*, Farnham, 2010.

Open University, *History of Architecture and Design, 1890–1939*, Milton Keynes, 1975.

Pile, John F., *Interior Design*, New Jersey, 2nd edn, 1995. A useful overview.

Schoeser, Mary, and Celia Rufey, *English and American Textiles: From 1871 to the Present*, London, 1989. An account of an often neglected aspect of interior design.

Sembach, Klaus-Jurgen, Gabriele Leuthauser and Peter Gossel, *Twentieth-Century Furniture Design*, Cologne, n.d. Informative survey of mainly German design.

Smith, C. Ray, *Interior Design in 20th-Century America: A History*, New York, 1987. General guide to recent American interior design.

Sparke, Penny, *Furniture*, London, 1986. An informative survey of popular and designer furniture.

——, *An Introduction to Design & Culture in the Twentieth Century*, London, 1986. Introduces the central issues of design history.

Taylor, Mark, and Julieanna Preston (eds), *Intimus: Interior Design Theory Reader*, Chichester, 2006. A useful collection of key writings about interior design.

Trocmé, Suzanne, *Influential Interiors: Shaping 20th Century Style, Key Interior Designers*, London, 1999. A general introduction to the interior design of the past century that concentrates on the work of the interior decorator.

Whitney Museum of American Art, *High Styles, Twentieth-Century American Design*, New York, 1986. Excellent source for Cranbrook Academy.

Chapter 1
Reforming Victorian Taste

Adburgham, Alison, *Shops and Shopping*, London, 1981.

Anscombe, Isabelle, and Charlotte Gere, *Arts and Crafts in Britain and America*, London, 1978.

Artistic Houses: Being a Series of Interior Views of a Number of the Most Beautiful and Celebrated Homes in the United States with a Description of the Art Treasures Contained Therein, 1st published New York, 1883, reprinted New York, 1971.

Aslin, Elizabeth, *The Aesthetic Movement: Prelude to Art Nouveau*, London, 1969.

Callen, Anthea, *Angel in the Studio: the Women of the Arts and Crafts Movement, 1870–1914*, London, 1978.

Cooper, Jeremy, *Victorian and Edwardian Furniture and Interiors, From the Gothic Revival to Art Nouveau*, London, New York, 1987.

Eastlake, C.L., *Hints on Household Taste*, London, Dover reprint, 1969.

Gere, Charlotte, *Nineteenth Century Decoration*, London, 1989.

Girouard, Mark, *Sweetness and Light*, Oxford, 1977.

Grier, Katherine C., *Culture and Comfort, People, Patrons and Upholstery, 1830–1930*, University of Massachusetts Press, 1988.

Lambourne, Lionel, *Utopian Craftsmen: the Arts and Crafts from the Cotswolds to Chicago*, London, 1980.

Miller, Michael, *The Bon Marché: Bourgeois Culture and the Department Store*, London, 1981.

Muthesius, Stefan, 'Why do we buy old furniture? Aspects of the antique in Britain, 1870–1910', *Art History*, Oxford, June 1988.

Naylor, Gillian, *The Arts and Crafts Movement: A Study of its Sources, Ideals and Influence on Design Theory*, London, 1971.

Service, Alastair, *Edwardian Interiors: Inside the Homes of the Poor, the Average and the Wealthy*, London, 1982.

Thornton, Peter, *Authentic Decor. The Domestic Interior 1620–1920*, London, 1984.

Chapter 2
The Search for a New Style

Billcliffe, Roger, *Charles Rennie Mackintosh: The Complete Furniture, Drawings and Interior Designs*, London, 1979.

Glasgow Museums and Art Galleries, *The Glasgow Style 1890–1920*, 1984.

Kallir, Jane, *Viennese Design and the Wiener Werkstätte*, London, 1986.

Kaufmann, E., '224 Avenue Louise', *Interiors*, February 1957, pp. 88–93.

Latham, Ian, *New Free Style*, London, 1980.

Levetus, A. S., 'Otto Prutscher: A Young Viennese Designer of Interiors', *The Studio*, Vol. xxxviii, pp. 33–41.

Madsen, S. T., 'Horta, Works and Style of Victor Horta before 1900', *Architectural Review*, 1955, pp. 388–92.

Nuttgens, Patrick, *Mackintosh and His Contemporaries*, London, 1988.

Pevsner, Nikolaus, 'George Walton. His Life and Work', *The Journal of the Royal Institute of British Architects*, vol. xlvi, 1939.

——, *Pioneers of Modern Design: From William Morris to Walter Gropius*, Harmondsworth, 3rd edn, 1975.

——, and J. M. Richards, *The Anti-Rationalists*, London, 1973.

Russell, Frank (ed.), *Art Nouveau Architecture*, London, 1979.

Schweiger, Werner J., *Wiener Werkstätte: Design in Vienna 1903–1932*, London, 1984.

Vergo, Peter, *Art in Vienna, 1898–1918*, London, 1975.

Chapter 3
The Modern Movement

Banham, Reyner, *Theory and Design in the First Machine Age*, London, 1960.

Besset, Maurice, *Le Corbusier: To Live with the Light*, London, 1978.

Blaser, Werner, *Mies van der Rohe, Furniture and Interiors*, London, 1982.

Bullock, Nicholas, 'First the Kitchen – then the Facade', *Journal of Design History*, Oxford, Vol. 1, Nos 3 and 4, 1988.

Corbusier, Le, *Towards a New Architecture*, London, Architectural Press reprint, 1970.

——,, *The City of Tomorrow*, London, Architectural Press reprint, 1971.

——, *The Decorative Art of Today*, London, Architectural Press reprint, 1987.

Faulkner, Thomas (ed.), *Design 1900–1960: Studies in Design and Popular Culture of the 20th Century*, Newcastle, 1976.

Heynen, Hilde, and Gülsüm Baydar (eds), *Negotiating Domesticity: Spatial Productions of Gender in Modern Architecture*, London, New York, 2005.

Hitchcock, Henry-Russell, and Philip Johnson, *The International Style*, London, New York, 1966.

Overy, Paul (et al.), *The Rietveld Schröder House*, London, 1988.

Overy, Paul, *De Stijl*, London, New York, 1991.

Rice, Charles, *The Emergence of the Interior: Architecture, Modernity, Domesticity*, London, New York, 2007.

Sparke, Penny, *The Modern Interior*, London, 2008.

Whitford, Frank, *The Bauhaus*, London, 1984.

Wilk, Christopher, *Marcel Breuer, Furniture and Interiors*, New York, 1981.

Willett, John, *The New Sobriety 1917–1933: Art and Politics in the Weimar Period*, London, 1978.

Wingler, Hans M., *Bauhaus*, Cambridge, Mass., 1969.

Yorke, F.R.S., and Frederick Gibberd, *The Modern Flat*, London, 3rd edn, 1950.

Chapter 4
Art Deco and the Moderne

Adam, Peter, *Eileen Gray: Architect, Designer: A Biography*, London, 1987.

Albrecht, Donald, *Designing Dreams, Modern Architecture in the Movies*, London, 1987.

Arts Council of Great Britain, *Thirties: British Art and Design before the War*, London, 1979.

Battersby, Martin, *The Decorative Twenties, The Decorative Thirties*, 2nd ed. rev. and ed. Philippe Garner, London, 1988.

Bayer, Patricia, *Art Deco Sourcebook: A Visual Reference to a Decorative Style 1920–1940*, Oxford, 1988.

——, *Art Deco Interiors: Decoration and Design Classics of the 1920s and 1930s*, London, New York, 1990.

Brunhammer, Yvonne, *Art Deco Style*, New York, 1984.

Camard, Florence, *Ruhlmann, Master of Art Deco*, London, 1982.

Davies, Karen, *At Home in Manhattan: Modern Decorative Arts, 1925 to the Depression*, New Haven, 1983.

Deslandres, Yvonne, *Paul Poiret*, London, 1987.

Duncan, Alastair (ed.), *Encyclopedia of Art Deco*, London, 1988.

Encyclopedie des Arts Décoratifs et Industriels Modernes au XXEME Siècle, London, New York, reprinted 1977.

Frankl, Paul T., *New Dimensions*, New York, 1928.

Gebhard, D., 'The Moderne in the US', *Architectural Association Quarterly*, London, July 1970.

Genaver, Emily, *Modern Interiors Today and Tomorrow*, New York, 1939.

Grief, M., *Depression Modern – The Thirties Style in America*, New York, 1975.

Massey, Anne, *Hollywood Beyond the Screen: Design and Material Culture*, Oxford, 2000.

Meikle, Jeffrey L., *Twentieth Century Limited: Industrial Design in America 1925–1939*, Philadelphia, 1979.

Richards, Jeffrey, *The Age of the Dream Palace; Cinema and Society in Britain 1930–1939*, London, 1984.

Sembach, Klaus-Jurgen, *Into the Thirties*, London, 1986.

Sharp, Denis, *The Picture Palace and Other Buildings for the Movies*, London, 1969.

Vellay, Marc, and Kenneth Frampton, *Pierre Chareau*, London, 1985.

Veronesi, Giulia, *Into the Twenties, Style and Design 1909–1929*, London, 1968.

Chapter 5
The Emergence of Interior Decoration as a Profession

Anscombe, Isabelle, *A Woman's Touch: Women in Design From 1860 to the Present Day*, London, 1984.

Baldwin, Billy, *Billy Baldwin Remembers*, New York, 1974.

Blake, Vernon, 'Morris, Munich & Cézanne, The Origin of the Modern French Decorators', *The Architectural Review*, April 1929, pp. 207–208.

Brown, Erica, *Sixty Years of Interior Design: The World of McMillen*, London, 1982.

Cornforth, John, *Inspiration of the Past*, Middlesex, 1985.

——, *The Search for a Style: Country Life and Architecture 1897–1935*, London, 1988.

De Wolfe, Elsie, *The House in Good Taste*, New York, 1913.

Draper, Dorothy, *Decorating is Fun! How to be Your Own Decorator*, New York, 1939.

Falke, Jacob von, *Art in the House: Historical, Critical and Aesthetical Studies on the Decoration and Furnishings of the Dwelling*, Boston, 1879.

Fisher, Richard B., *Syrie Maugham*, London, 1978.

Green, Harvey, *The Light of the Home: An Intimate View of the Lives of Women in Victorian America*, New York, 1983.

Hicks, David, *Style and Design*, Middlesex, 1987.

Potvin, John, *Bachelors of a Different Sort: Queer Aesthetics, Material Culture and the Modern Interior in Britain*, Manchester, 2014.

Simpson, Colin, *The Artful Partners: The Secret Association of Bernard Berenson and Joseph Duveen*, London, 1987.

Smith, Jane S., *Elsie de Wolfe*, New York, 1982.

Sparke, Penny, *Elsie de Wolfe: The Birth of Modern Interior Decoration*, New York, 2005.

Throop, Lucy Abbot, *Furnishing the Home of Good Taste: A Brief Sketch of the Period Styles in*

Interior Decoration With Suggestions as to Their Employment in the Homes of Today, New York, 1912.

Wharton, Edith, and Codman Ogden, Jnr, *The Decoration of Houses*, 1902, reprinted with additions, New York, 1978.

Wheeler, Candace Thrubber, *Principles of Home Decoration, With Practical Examples*, New York, 1903.

Chapter 6
Post-war Modernism

Banham, Reyner, *New Brutalism: Ethic or Aesthetic?*, London, 1966.

Casson, Hugh (ed.), *Inscape, The Design of Interiors*, London, 1968.

Duffy, F., and C. Cave, 'Bürolandschaft, an Appraisal', *Planning Office Space*, ed. F. Duffy, C. Cave and J. Worthington, London, 1976.

Eudes, Georges, *Modern French Interiors*, Paris, 1959.

Garrett, Stephen, 'Interior Design', *Design*, London, August 1959.

ILEA, *Utility Furniture and Fashion*, London, 1974.

Jackson, Lesley, 'Contemporary Architecture' and *Interiors of the 1950s*, London, 1994.

Jencks, Charles, *Modern Movements in Architecture*, Middlesex, 1973.

Kaufmann, E., *What is Modern Interior Design?*, Museum of Modern Art, New York, 1953.

McFadden, D. E. (ed.), *Scandinavian Modern Design, 1880–1980*, New York, 1982.

Pulos, Arthur J., *The American Design Adventure, 1940–1975*, Cambridge, Mass., 1988.

Till, Jeremy, *Architecture Depends*, Cambridge, Mass., 2013.

Weller, John, 'The British Institute of Interior Design', *DIA Yearbook*, London, 1976.

Chapter 7
Consumer Culture

Attfield, Judy, *Bringing Modernity Home: Writings on Popular Design and Material Culture*, Manchester, 2007.

Bayley, Stephen (et al.), ''60s Remembered', *Designers' Journal*, London, May 1988, pp. 51–59.

Bourdieu, Pierre, *Distinction*, London, 1979.

Brutton, M., 'Review of Postwar British Design', *Design*, London, January 1970.

Conran, Terence, *Terence Conran on Design*, London, New York, 1996.

Derieux, Mary, and Isabelle Stevenson,

The Complete Book of Interior Decorating, New York, 1956.

Favata, Ignazia, *Joe Colombo and Italian Design of the Sixties*, London, 1988.

Goldstein, Carolyn M., *Do It Yourself: Home Improvement in 20th Century America*, New York, 1998.

Hebdige, Dick, *Subculture: The Meaning of Style*, London, 1979.

Hine, Thomas, *Populuxe*, New York, 1987.

Horn, Richard, *Fifties Style: Then and Now*, New York, 1985.

Lee, Martyn. J. (ed), *The Consumer Society Reader*, Oxford, Malden, Mass., 2000.

Mackenzie, Dorothy, *Green Design: Design for the Environment*, London, 2nd edn, 1997.

Massey, Anne, *The Independent Group: Modernism and Mass Culture in Britain, 1945–59*, Manchester, New York, 1995.

Miller, Daniel, Peter Jackson, Nigel Thrift, Beverley Holbrook and Michael Rowlands, *Shopping, Place and Identity*, London, New York, 1998.

Phillips, Barty, *Conran and the Habitat Story*, London, 1984.

Pilatowicz, Graznya, *Eco-Interiors: A Guide to Environmentally Conscious Interior Design*, New York, 1995.

Renzio, Toni del, 'Shoes, Hair and Coffee', *ARK*, London, Autumn 1957.

Riesman, David, *The Lonely Crowd*, New Haven, 1950.

Shurka, Norma, and Orberto Gili, *Underground Interiors: Decorating for Alternate Life Styles*, London, 1972.

Sparke, Penny (ed.), *Did Britain Make It? British Design in Context, 1946–86*, London, 1986.

Vale, Brenda and Robert, *Green Architecture: Design for a Sustainable Future*, London, Boston, 1991.

Whiteley, Nigel, *Pop Design: Modernism to Mod*, London, 1987.

Yeang, Ken, *Designing with Nature: The Ecological Basis for Architectural Design*, London, New York, 1995.

Chapter 8
The Post-modern Era

Banham, Reyner, *Contemporary Architecture of Japan, 1958–1984*, London, 1985.

Baudrillard, Jean, *The System of Objects*, London, New York, 1996.

Buchanan, Peter, 'The Nostalgic Now: Flyte, Fellini and Ferlinghetti', *Architectural Review*, London, January 1988.

Davey, Peter (ed.), 'Interior Spaces', *Architectural Review*, January 1989.

'Deconstruction in Architecture', *Architectural Design*, London, Vol. 58, No. 3/4, 1988.

Frow, John, *Time and Commodity Culture: Essays in Cultural Theory and Postmodernity*, Oxford, New York, 1997.

Gardner, Carl, and Julie Sheppard, *Consuming Passion: The Rise of Retail Culture*, London, 1989.

Hatje, Gerd, and Herbert Weisskamp, *Rooms by Design: Houses, Apartments, Studios, Lofts*, London, 1989.

Jencks, Charles, *The Language of Post-Modern Architecture*, London, 1977.

——, and George Baird (eds), *Meaning in Architecture*, London, 1970.

Knobel, Lance, *International Interiors*, London, 1988.

Kroa, Joan, and Suzanne Slesin, *Hi-Tech: The Industrial Style and Source Book for the Home*, New York, 1978.

Matrix, *Making Space: Women and the Man-made Environment*, London, 1984.

McDermott, Catherine, *Street Style: British Design in the 80s*, Design Council, London, 1987.

Myerson, Jeremy, *International Interiors 5*, London, 1995.

Raymond, Santa, and Roger Cunliffe, *Tomorrow's Office: Creating Effective and Humane Interiors*, London, New York, 1997.

Sarup, Madan, *Identity, Culture and the Postmodern World*, Edinburgh, Athens, Georgia, 1996, reprinted 1998.

Sparke, Penny, *Italian Design*, London, 1988.

Thackara, John (ed.), *Design After Modernism*, London, 1988.

Venturi, Robert, *Complexity and Contradiction in Architecture*, New York, 1974.

——, *Learning From Las Vegas*, Cambridge, Mass., 1979.

Chapter 9
The Sustainability of Interior Design

Brooker, Graeme, and Sally Stone, *Rereadings: Interior Architecture and the Design Principles of Remodelling Existing Buildings*, London, 2004.

Chapman, Jonathan, *Emotionally Durable Design: Objects, Experiences and Empathy*, London, 2005.

Farmer, John, and Kenneth Richardson (ed.), *Green Shift: Changing Attitudes in Architecture to the Natural World*, Oxford, 1999.

Fuad-Luke, Alistair, *The Eco-Design Handbook: A Complete Sourcebook for the Home and Office*, London, 2nd rev. edn, 2005.

Hagan, Susannah, *Taking Shape: A New Contract between Architecture and Nature*, Oxford, Boston, 2001.

Pearman, H., and A. Whalley, *The Architecture of Eden*, London, 2003.

Sanders, Joel, 'Curtain Wars: Architects, Decorators and the Twentieth-century Domestic Interior', *Harvard Design Magazine*, 16, 2002, pp. 1–9.

Chapter 10
Transnational Interiors

Herz, Manuel, *African Modernism: The Architecture of Independence: Ghana, Senegal, Côte d'Ivoire, Kenya, Zambia*, Zurich, 2015.

Huppatz, D.J., *Modern Asian Design*, London, 2018.

Jacobs, Jane and Cairns, Stephen 'The Modern Touch: Interior Design and Modernization of Post-independent Singapore', *Environment and Planning A*, 40, 2008, pp. 572–95.

Jones, Robin '"Thinking" the Domestic Interior in Postcolonial South Asia: The Home of Geoffrey Bawa in Sri Lanka, 1960 to 1998', *Interiors: Design, Architecture, Culture*, 3: 3, 203–26.

Kikuchi, Yuko, and Yunah Lee, 'Transnational Modern Design Histories in East Asia: AnIntroduction, *Journal of Design History*, 27: 4, 2014, pp. 323–34.

Kirkham, Pat, and Susan Weber (eds), *History of Design: Decorative Arts and Material Culture, 1400–2000*, New Haven and London, 2013.

Lees-Maffei, Grace, and Kjetil Fallan (eds), *Designing Worlds: National Design Histories in an Age of Globalisation,* New York and Oxford, 2016.

Patel, Dhara 'The Evolution of Elite High-Rise Condominiums in India: From the Global to the Neo-colonial?', *Postcolonial Studies*, 20: 4, 2017, pp. 456–78.

Acknowledgments

I would like to thank the following, without whom this book would not have been possible: Catherine McDermott, Penny Sparke, Stephen Hayward, Stuart Evans, Jacqueline Thwaites, David Prestage, Paul Greenhalgh, Gwen Carr, Harry Massey, Judith Massey, Robert Massey, the staff at the Cooper-Hewitt Museum, New York Public Library, the Parsons School of Design library, the National Art Library at the Victoria and Albert Museum, London, Kingston University Library and Crawley Public Library.

Sources of Illustrations

Index

"This kind of book at this kind of price
is what art publishing should be about"
—*New York Times Book Review*

"An extraordinarily rich and varied series"
—Linda Nochlin

The World of Art series is a comprehensive,
accessible, indispensable companion to the history
of art and its latest developments, covering themes,
artists and movements that span centuries and
the gamut of visual culture around the globe.

You may also like:

Art Deco
Alastair Duncan

Bauhaus
Frank Whitford

Charles Rennie Mackintosh
Alan Crawford

The Language of Ornament
James Trilling

World of Art

For more information about
Thames & Hudson, and the World of Art
series, visit **thamesandhudsonusa.com**